YOU CAN DO IT

A PR Skills Manual for Librarians

by
RITA KOHN
and
KRYSTA TEPPER

The Scarecrow Press, Inc.
Metuchen, N.J., & London
1981

Library of Congress Cataloging in Publication Data

Kohn, Rita T
  You can do it.

  Bibliography: p.
  Includes index.
  1. Public relations--Libraries--Handbooks, manuals,
etc. I. Tepper, Krysta, joint author. II. Title.
Z716.3.K64   021.7   80-24217
ISBN 0-8108-1401-3

To

Howard and Walter

and

Tom, Martin and Sharon

CONTENTS

ACKNOWLEDGMENTS

We are grateful to the Staff and Board members of the Corn Belt Library System (Illinois) Member Libraries for their encouragement throughout the years of "bringing PR/publicity into the open." Special thanks go to Jane Broeksmit and Anne Martin of Dwight for their excellent suggestions regarding the final manuscript and to Patrick D. McCowan of Normal and Ulrich Wehrli of Bern, Switzerland for their contributions to the content of the manuscript. A word of appreciation is due to the Staff of the Schweizer Bibliothekdienst and the Berner Volksbücherei of Bern, Switzerland for their assistance and sharing. To our families go our utmost acknowledgment for their selflessness during the months when idea led to action and action yielded to single-minded purpose: the production of a tool that will be of value to the librarians who have the basic responsibility of selling the library and all it has to offer. This is our way of saying "thank you" to a giving profession.

Rita Kohn
Normal, Illinois

Krysta Tepper
Bloomington, Illinois

December 1979

LIST OF ILLUSTRATIONS

INTRODUCTION

Your community is spending a sizeable sum of money to house, furnish, supply and staff a library. It is important how that library looks on the outside and on the inside. It is important how that library, as a physical and community service entity, presents itself to the public that supports it. It is important how the various populations of your community perceive the library building, its materials and its services. What image do you project?

Your reaching out to the public should reflect the professional service you give. Signs that look as if you made them in a hurry while talking on the telephone, hastily scrawled flyers on weak ditto sheets, "Tuesday" when you mean "Thursday" in a newspaper story make people wonder if the program you're advertising is any good or if the library can deliver what it promises.

This workbook is designed to help you sharpen the skills necessary to make the library attractive, functional and competitive in a highly visual society. This program will require a commitment of time and of money for the needed supplies.

Work at each skill until you feel comfortable with it and then move on. You may not need each skill in the order in which it has been presented, so skip around and adapt the material to your advantage. As you complete a step, evaluate and enjoy the results. The praise from pleased patrons, board members and fellow staff members will let you know that meaningful public relations is noticeable.

Even though you may have been skeptical at first, in the end you will have proved that you can do it ... you can make your library, its materials and its services be good and look good. You can project an up-to-date library image.

PART I: FINDING OUT ABOUT YOUR LIBRARY

INTRODUCTION

A delivery man drove up and down the main street of the small community when finally, on his third trip past, the librarian came out and flagged him down. He had no idea which of the buildings was the library. It had no sign identifying it.

A new resident, who knew from the sign that the library opened at 1:00 pm, arrived promptly, but sat in her car for ten minutes waiting for someone to open the door. Finally, she decided to try it. To her amazement, the door opened, to reveal a librarian busily working behind her desk. From the outside, to a newcomer, the drawn bamboo curtains had given the impression of a locked facility not yet open for business. She soon learned that the curtains are never opened--the sun would ruin the book jackets!

Visitors driving through a community couldn't find the antique shop they were seeking, so they stopped at the building marked "Public Library." They asked for and got directions.

Vacationers, on their way through a middle-sized city, were intrigued by a banner across a modern building--BOOKS ARE LIFELONG FRIENDS: ENTER. They parked, entered and spent two very nice hours browsing. They brought home a handful of ideas for their own librarian.

WHEN WAS THE LAST TIME THAT YOU APPROACHED YOUR LIBRARY AS A PASSERBY OR AS A NEW RESIDENT? The steps that follow are designed to help you make your library inviting from the outside.

STEP 1: TAKE INVENTORY OF THE OUTSIDE OF THE BUILDING.

Check out both the front door and the parking door entrances (and any others your particular building may have) during evening and daytime hours.

YES NO

____ ____   a.   The library is visibly identified with a sign that says "LIBRARY."

____ ____   b.   The library's sign is comparable to, compatible with and competitive with the signs of local businesses.

____ ____   c.   The sign is shabby.

1

____ ____   d.   Library hours are clearly posted.

____ ____   e.   Library hours are hand printed on a piece of shirt cardboard. The lettering is fading.

____ ____   f.   Library hours are on a 'stick on sign.' Letters and numbers keep falling off.

____ ____   g.   An attractive window display shows library materials of current interest.

____ ____   h.   Curtains facing outside windows are faded and fraying.

____ ____   i.   Windows are partially covered with backs of shelves.

____ ____   j.   There is attractive landscaping on the library grounds.

____ ____   k.   The planter adds the right touch of color.

____ ____   l.   The shrubs need trimming.

____ ____   m.   The library looks open when it is open.

____ ____   n.   The rock garden really looks good.

____ ____   o.   The sidewalk is cracked and crumbly.

____ ____   p.   The sidewalks and parking areas are cleared of ice and snow.

____ ____   q.   Snow is piled every-which-way. At least five parking spaces are lost as a result.

____ ____   r.   Leaves have been raked and removed.

____ ____   s.   Several lightbulbs are burned out--outside and inside the building.

____ ____   t.   The entranceway is dark.

____ ____   u.   The parking area is well paved.

____ ____   v.   The green areas in the parking lot are doing well.

____ ____   w.   The doors open without brute force.

STEP 2: ASSESS YOUR INVENTORY.

Got the Picture? Is your building on the outside such that a person walking by wants to come in? Make a list of the improvements needed as a report to your library board at its next meeting or today, whichever is sooner.

1.   Make a list of plus items and give praise to whom it is due:

LIST OF PLUS ITEMS   SAY "THANK YOU" TO: JOB DONE

_____   _____   _____

2.   Make a list of improvements needed and decide who will make them.
     Give some thought to priorities.

FOR LIBRARIAN ACTION   FOR BOARD ACTION OR LIBRARIAN ACTION

List of Improvements Needed	Who Will Make Them	Estimated Cost	Time Schedule	Job Done
_____	_____	_____	_____	_____
_____	_____	_____	_____	_____

3.   Follow up on the lists.   Make sure things are completed.

4.   Make a note of any differences the above actions make.   Report to your
     board.   Share your ideas and successes with other librarians through
     your state library or system newsletter, short articles to professional
     journals and "show and tell" at library meetings.

     "It makes you feel at home.   You don't feel like you're intruding. "
These are the comments of one young library patron when she spoke of her
library.   The atmosphere, she explained, is created by plants placed all
around, easy chairs in clusters for relaxing reading and a general brightness
because of the decor and color scheme.   The attitude of the library personnel is equally easy-going and cheerful.

     One patron, leaving a newly built library, noticed a woman wandering
about the corridor adjacent to the parking lot.   "How do I get to where the
books are?" asked the woman.   Why couldn't she figure out how to get
there?   Directly to the left of the entrance is a door marked "Community
Room. "   Directly to the right are doors marked "Ladies" and "Gentlemen. "
On the far wall are two doors, one marked "Exit, " the other "Staff Only";
both go to the same corridor leading to offices.   The flight of stairs past
the rest rooms appears to end in a brick wall.   "I'm looking for a sign
that says: 'This way to the library. '   I knew my way around the old library, " explained the woman, "I do miss it. "

     A doll-house became the absolute fascination for a four-year-old and
resulted in continuous visits to the Children's Department of that library.
Books were read to the doll-house people, stories were told to them, pup-
pet plays were created for them.   That four-year-old has grown up into a
young man who retains a great love for libraries because there was that
something special just for him during a formative part of his life.

     WHEN WAS THE LAST TIME YOU LOOKED AROUND YOUR LIBRARY

AS IF YOU WERE ANY ONE OF A NUMBER OF KINDS OF PEOPLE WHO COULD USE IT? The steps that follow are designed to help you make your library inviting on the inside.

STEP 3: TAKE INVENTORY OF THE INSIDE OF YOUR BUILDING.

Check out impressions from all entrances. Walk in as a patron would.

YES NO

____ ____ a. Signs in the entranceway read "NO TELEPHONE CALLS PERMITTED," "NOT A PUBLIC TOILET FACILITY" or other similar NO or NOT messages.

____ ____ b. Attractive signs in the entranceway announce upcoming library programs.

____ ____ c. There are two bulletin boards--one for general information, the other for library announcements.

____ ____ d. There's a well-planned display in the entranceway.

____ ____ e. There's a happy look about the check-out area.

____ ____ f. The check-out area looks like a flea market.

____ ____ g. A floor plan is easily visible and easy to follow.

____ ____ h. The card catalog is within immediate sight.

____ ____ i. Shelves and contents are identified at five feet from the floor, a comfortable height for both tall and short patrons. (Try it out....)

____ ____ j. Low shelves have displays on the topmost shelf.

____ ____ k. The library is orderly but not antiseptic.

____ ____ l. Books are jammed into shelves whichever way they'll fit.

____ ____ m. Reading and browsing clusters have comfortable chairs and good lighting.

____ ____ n. There's a sturdy papier-mâché animal at the children's department entrance. The young ones can climb on it safely.

____ ____ o. Fire exit signs are posted at a height so that all patrons can see them. The path is clear to the doors.

____ ____ p. Carpeting is frayed in spots. If people watch their steps, heels won't get caught in the loose threads.

YES   NO

____ ____   q.   The fifth grade class in 1960 made that adorable sign for the then new record collection. Too bad it got shabby (the sign, not the collection).

____ ____   r.   The signs all over are sloppy, now that we notice them.

____ ____   s.   Here it is March 20th already and the valentine card display is still up (or something similar in time sequence).

____ ____   t.   There is a very clear pattern of traffic from the entrance-way to the information desk.

____ ____   u.   Each area is clearly marked in a way that's inviting to anyone. (Examples: CHILDREN'S DEPARTMENT, LISTENING CENTER, REFERENCE)

____ ____   v.   Art objects are an integral part of the library's arrangement.

____ ____   w.   Live plants or a cactus garden or an aquarium, etc., are in the library to add that special touch.

____ ____   x.   Is that first impression a pleasant one?

____ ____   y.   Are materials easily accessible? Are they logically placed? (Readers' Guide ... near the Periodicals? Globe and maps near TRAVEL?)

STEP 4:   ASSESS YOUR INVENTORY.

1.   Make a list of things that make your library look and feel good:

LIST OF PLUS ITEMS   SAY THANK YOU TO: JOB DONE

_____

_____

_____

_____

_____

_____

2.   Make a list of things to do to improve the first impression. Number these items according to a priority rating:

FOR LIBRARIAN ACTION	FOR BOARD OR LIBRARIAN ACTION			
List of Improvements Needed	Who Will Make Them	Estimated Cost	Time Schedule	Job Done

_____

_____

_____

_____

_____

_____

3.   Follow up on the lists.   Make sure things are completed.

4.   Make a note of any differences the above actions make.   Report to your board.   Share your ideas and successes.

STEP 5:   ASSESS THE ARCHITECTURAL STYLE OF YOUR BUILDING IN ITS SETTING.

Determining the interior character and exterior style of your library will help you in all the following steps that comprise a pr/p program.

<u>Exterior of the Library</u>

Is your library a(n):

_____   store front
_____   Carnegie building
_____   library building other than Carnegie architecture (specify:_____)
_____   expanded aluminum storage building
_____   pre-fab house modified as a library facility
_____   shared facility (inside a school, community building, business, church, home)
_____   renovated building (Church, school, home, railroad depot, firehouse, business)
_____   (other)_____

Is your library:

_____   surrounded by a park or green area   _____   part of a civic complex
_____   surrounded by businesses (downtown)   _____   off by itself
_____   connected with other buildings   _____   in the inner city
_____   in an industrial zone   _____   in the suburbs
_____   in a shopping mall   _____   in a rural area
_____   (other)_____

Is the architectural style of the exterior of your library:

____ modern	____ French
____ Colonial	____ Italian
____ Mediterranean	____ Spanish
____ Carnegie	____ Georgian
____ (other)_____	

Interior of the Library

Different areas within the library can have differing atmospheres created through the furnishings. List the areas that fit the descriptions listed below. What factors make each section take on that atmosphere? List them:

DESCRIPTION   AREA   FACTORS

informal	_____	_____
quaint	_____	_____
friendly	_____	_____
sophisticated	_____	_____
grand	_____	_____
contemporary	_____	_____
intimidating	_____	_____
youthful	_____	_____
playful	_____	_____
humorous	_____	_____
homespun	_____	_____
dignified	_____	_____
ornate	_____	_____
turn-of-the-century	_____	_____
somber	_____	_____
serious	_____	_____
cluttered	_____	_____
barren	_____	_____
musty	_____	_____
bewildering	_____	_____
nondescript	_____	_____
(other)	_____	_____

AN ASIDE

FURNISHINGS include the ceiling, flooring, wall covering (texture and color), furniture and fixtures (lights, switches, door handles).

ATMOSPHERE is attained by an integrated relationship of details--lines, scales, masses, color and surface treatments.

FUNCTIONAL AND PSYCHOLOGICAL PURPOSES of each area dictate the furnishings.

GOOD COLOR COMPOSITION requires that large areas be painted neutralized colors. Small areas can be painted in more intense colors (or papered, if preferred).

FURNITURE can be standard library designs, can be specially designed or can be home or office furniture integrated into the overall design.

VISITS to a variety of other libraries can yield limitless ideas for your own library.

Jot down ideas and places to visit:

The first thing I noticed about this library was how crowded it felt. Books were jammed into shelves every which way, baskets of paperbacks and magazines and boxes of patterns were placed around any available floor space. Chairs looked too big for the spots they were pushed into. I always felt uncomfortable--not welcome, just claustrophobic. Months later, I went back. I couldn't believe the difference. That same place looked spacious! How could that happen?

One architectural firm spent as much time choosing the furnishings as it did in creating the layout. In doing both, the firm used the results of a community survey (with questions on interior design built into the instrument) and incorporated the ideas and questions of all library staff members. The result is a place that really looks and is "put together with people, use and staff in mind."

"Effective use of space promotes positive PR," stated the workshop speaker, but no one present believed her until she showed each participant how to measure floor space on a graph-grid, how to fit cut-out furnishings on the graph as they appear in reality, and how to manipulate those cut-outs to get different floor plans before actually shoving furniture around and not have it work. Each participant marked in electrical outlets, the swing of each door, space for maneuvering wheelchairs and baby strollers, intensity of sun during specific hours of the day, special safety factors to consider, accessibility for specific groups, supervision needs, etc., and worked with these factors in the placement of departments and their furnishings.

The need for more space was recognized by the library board so they contracted for the building to be enlarged. After the construction took place the board allocated money for furniture. It turned out what they needed didn't fit into the space.

The interior structure of the library was remodeled according to what the board believed to be the needs to improve business. Despite the large expenditure of money and a lot of publicity, business didn't increase. A consultant was then called in and she did a community survey (one had not been done before). She found that the make-up of the community had changed considerably; the data on which the board had relied were outdated. Thus, there wasn't a clientele present to respond to the renovation.

STEP 6: HOW TO MAKE AND USE A FLOOR PLAN OF YOUR LIBRARY.

See the graph and patterns of furnishings on pages 10 and 11. Each piece of furniture and equipment is made to the scale of $\frac{1}{4}$ inch equals 1 foot. The graph is the same scale.

1. Measure the dimensions of your room. Outline the size of the room on graph paper.

2. Note the permanent fixtures on your graph:

   windows   electrical outlets
   doors (swing direction)   heat registers
   hearth   fire exits

   Your floor plan must be made around them.

3. Cut out the patterns for the furniture and equipment you have, or are buying. Arrange them within the limits of your room.

4. For permanent copies of your floor plan, trace (or paste) the patterns on $\frac{1}{4}$" graph paper.

SUGGESTIONS FOR FURNITURE PLACEMENT:

1. The circulation desk is within immediate sight.

2. The card catalog is easily visible after entering.

3. Related areas are close to each other with each area clearly identified.

4. There is easy visual and functional control.

5. There is space to carry on the types of programs your library has developed--story hours, local history, film showing, crafts, etc.

6. Work and storage areas are included.

STEP 7: A MINI-SURVEY: QUESTIONS TO ANSWER YOURSELF.

Do you (and your staff):

____ know just about all of your patrons
____ recognize and acknowledge a few
____ know absolutely no one by name

Is your clientele (determine percentage through government statistics):

____ transitory
____ stable

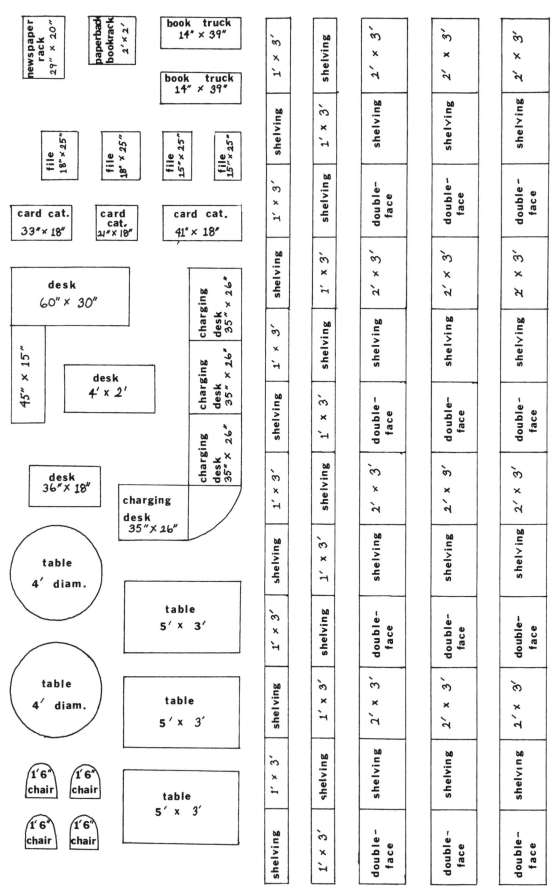

1. Patterns of Furniture

_____ very young children whose parents bring them and stay with them at
the library
_____ very young children who are dropped off to remain on their own at the
library
_____ school age children coming in classes with teachers
_____ school age children coming on their own after school
_____ children coming to special programs but not checking out books
_____ senior citizens coming for programs put on by another agency in a library room
_____ people coming in to read papers and magazines, not checking anything out
_____ people out of jobs needing a lot of assistance (GED, CLEP, retraining)
_____ people wanting recreational materials
_____ people wanting audio-visual materials
_____ people who come on a specific schedule as part of their routine
_____ people in retirement
_____ handicapped individuals
_____ (other)_____
_____ employed by one major employer
_____ employed by diversified employers
_____ employed outside of the community
_____ skilled
_____ unskilled
_____ professional

Your community, as a whole:

_____ uses the library and is vocal about library issues
_____ never complains and never asks for much
_____ hardly knows the library is there

What motivates people to come to your library? (Verify this section against
the sections above. Do they mesh?):

_____ pleasure reading
_____ work related
_____ continuing education
_____ hobbies
_____ school work
_____ to attend programs
_____ to use non-book materials
_____ reference

_____ magazines and newspapers
_____ to socialize
_____ do-it-yourself data
_____ to view exhibits that are publicized
_____ to use special collections
_____ to bring children
_____ to check telephone directories
_____ (other)_____

Your library staff:

_____ doesn't get involved with politics
_____ invites local and state officials for special events or to just stop by
_____ generates outreach activities
_____ doesn't have time to visit schools, nursing homes, etc.
_____ has good contact with all of the other service agencies in the area

____ maintains branches in hospitals, jails, YM, YW and other institutions
or civic centers in the area
____ does periodic user surveys
____ doesn't know how much of the population has library cards
____ attends library board meetings
____ is never in on any decision making regarding the library
____ has a working knowledge of standards of library service
____ is thoroughly familiar with library board policy
____ knows the library board's philosophy of service

STEP 8: A COMMUNITY SURVEY.

This is a sample survey that can be mailed or delivered to everyone
or sent randomly to every 10th or 15th or 25th (etc.) person in your community. A good layout is to fit it on a sheet $8\frac{1}{2}$" x 14" with all of the questions on one side. On the other side, the bottom third has your return address and pre-paid postage printed. The top third has the mailing address
of the recipient. Thus, the questionnaire can be refolded, stapled and mailed
back to the library by the person who fills out the questionnaire.

Month, day, year

Dear Resident of *_____:

We will greatly appreciate your taking a few minutes of your time to fill out
the following answers to questions about the library in *_____. Because
we want to provide library programs to serve the community, we need your
help in establishing priorities and guidelines.

1. How important is the library in community life in *_____?
    very important ____ moderately important ____ not very important ____
    completely unimportant ____

2. How important do you think the library should be in *_____?
    very important ____ moderately important ____ not very important ____
    completely unimportant ____

3. What kinds of library activities seem to be most readily available to you
    (and your children) in *_____?
    _____

4. What kinds of library activities have you participated in or enjoyed?
    _____

5. What are your favorite hobbies and pastimes?
    _____

_____
*Fill in the name of your community.

6. About how many times in the past year have you done the following? (circle the best response)

a. called the library for information   0 1 2 3 4   5 6 7 8   9 10 11 12 over 12
b. gone to the library for a book   0 1 2 3 4   5 6 7 8   9 10 11 12 over 12
c. taken your children to a story
       hour   0 1 2 3 4   5 6 7 8   9 10 11 12 over 12
d. gone to a lecture or slide show
       at the library   0 1 2 3 4   5 6 7 8   9 10 11 12 over 12
e. read the library newsletter   0 1 2 3 4   5 6 7 8   9 10 11 12 over 12
f. gone to a crafts class at the li-
       brary   0 1 2 3 4   5 6 7 8   9 10 11 12 over 12
g. gone to the library to read
       magazines or newspapers   0 1 2 3 4   5 6 7 8   9 10 11 12 over 12
h. gone to the library for informa-
       tion   0 1 2 3 4   5 6 7 8   9 10 11 12 over 12
i. borrowed films or recordings
       from the library   0 1 2 3 4   5 6 7 8   9 10 11 12 over 12

7. From your point of view, what kinds of library activities seem to be most needed in *_____?

_____

8. Please indicate whether you agree or disagree with the following statements:

		agree	disagree
a.	I don't know much about the library in *_____		
b.	There aren't enough library activities in *_____		
c.	Library events are usually at the wrong time		
d.	If I knew more about when library events were happening, I would probably go more		
e.	If the library were more informal I might go more		
f.	I would rather buy my books at the bookstore		
g.	The library is an important part of *_____'s history		
h.	The library is too far away		
i.	The library is important for children in *_____		

9. Have you heard about the different library services in *_____?
     yes ____   no ____

10. We would like some information about you:

     Zip code: _____   Sex: male ____   female ____
     Marital status: _____   Occupation: _____
     Do you have school age children living at home? ____ Ages: _____
     How long have you lived in *_____? _____
     Age: under 18 ____ 18-25 ____ 26-40 ____ 41-65 ____ over 65 ____
     Education: grade school ____ high school ____ some college ____
       college degree ____ graduate degree ____ vocational training ____

Thank you very much for your help in filling out this questionnaire. It will be reviewed, and your recommendations and opinions will be carefully considered. If you would like to know more about the Library of *_____, please write your name and address below:

PLEASE REFOLD WITH THE LIBRARY'S NAME AND ADDRESS SHOWING AND SEAL THE EDGES. POSTAGE HAS BEEN PRE-PAID, SO JUST DROP THIS COMPLETED QUESTIONNAIRE IN A MAIL BOX.

STEP 9: LIST THE SERVICES YOU ARE PROVIDING AND WANT TO PROVIDE FOR YOUR COMMUNITY. (Based on determined needs and interests).

Note How Well Known These Are To The Publics You Serve.

BASIC SERVICES   DEGREE OF USER AWARENESS   MEASURING TOOL

_____

_____

_____

_____

_____

_____

_____

ADDITIONAL SERVICES DEGREE OF USER AWARENESS MEASURING TOOL

_____

_____

_____

_____

STEP 10: REVIEW THE WRITTEN LIBRARY BOARD POLICY IN LIGHT OF THE ATTITUDES AND NEEDS OF YOUR COMMUNITY AS DETERMINED BY STUDIES.

Make a list of the nitty-gritty items to talk over with your staff and board:

POINTS FOR DISCUSSION	ACTION TO TAKE	BY WHOM	TIME SCHEDULE	JOB DONE

STEP 11: REVIEW THE DEGREE OF COOPERATION THAT EXISTS BETWEEN YOUR LIBRARY AND OTHER LIBRARIES IN YOUR COMMUNITY.

List the other libraries in your community:

NAME	MAJOR FUNCTION	LIBRARIAN	TEL. #

Do you share:

LIST IDEAS OF WHAT YOU CAN DO IN EACH AREA:

____ expensive reference materials

____ standard catalogs

____ A-V materials

____ periodicals

____ staff expertise

____ cooperative collection development

____ programs

____ exhibits, displays

____ news media coverage

____ ideas

____ reciprocal facilities

<u>Do you have</u>:

____ an informal cooperative arrange-   _____
      ment   _____
____ a formal cooperative arrange-   _____
      ment   _____

<u>Do the ...</u>

____ staffs know each other   _____
____ governing bodies have contact   _____
____ people in the community know   _____
      about the cooperative arrange-   _____
      ments and how to use them   _____

Outline a program of how you could effectively work with other libraries in your area. Could you share staffing, could you write joint program proposals for grants, etc.? Follow up with action and board approval.

SUMMARY: PART I

By determining the interior character and exterior style of your library you can design signs and all other publicity materials in keeping with that character and style.

By identifying the publics that you serve, and need to serve, you can create the kind of atmosphere that correctly reflects your community. It is this compatible atmosphere that you want to advertise. When your library promotionals are properly directed the residents of your community will relate to them and will use the library fully.

It is this atmosphere of the library that either brings in or keeps people out. It is the library staff's ability to effectively interpret the collection to users that keeps people coming. A good product, properly publicized, should be the basic aim of every library board. Advertising can't and shouldn't be expected to be used as a cover-up for a poor situation. A librarian must use public relations/publicity skills along with providing the finest kind of library services and materials your citizens deserve.

Work on!

PART II: SIGNS IDENTIFYING THE LIBRARY BUILDING

STEP 12: YOU NEED AN OUTSIDE SIGN FOR THE LIBRARY. HOW DO YOU PROCEED?

1. Locate sign-making sources (make a list of names, addresses, comments):

    a. Check the yellow pages of the telephone directory.
    b. Ask around. Check these sources against what you already have.
    c. Look at buildings. Which signs catch your fancy? Find out who put them up. Add these sources to your list.
    d. Check out trade classes in area schools. Do they have special projects?

2. Investigate the sign-making sources:

    a. Ask the sources on your list to show you what is available.
    b. Visit sites where each kind of sign is already installed.
    c. Ask questions and make notes:

COMPANY	ADDRESS	DESCRIPTION OF SIGN	COSTS: INSTALLATION /UPKEEP	GOOD/BAD POINTS

3. Determine the factors regarding the design of your sign (Review Step 5):

    a. Style of the building
    b. Distance from which sign must be seen
    c. Styles of other signs in the area
    d. Placement of the sign
    e. Number of signs needed to effectively identify the library from all sides
    f. Weather conditions
    g. Budget for installation and upkeep
    h. Insurance and Liability
    i. Safety
    j. How soon you need the sign

4. Make a check list of your preferences:

    a. Size (consider scale relationships to building, placement and land-
            scaping)
    b. Lettering (whatever style you choose, be certain it is easy to read
            and identifies the library)
    c. Materials (this is wide-open; money and your imagination are the
            limits--possibilities include stained glass, neon, attached
            lettering, chiseled into stone, paint on any surface, reflect-
            ing so as to be seen at night ...)
    d. Placement (if near bushes, keep bushes trimmed so signs can be
            seen--keep this in mind for budget needs; can be free-stand-
            ing or attached to the building; can be near the building or
            near the street or sidewalk ...)
    e. Color(s) (use in a way that creates interest and a positive identifi-
            cation)
    f. Message (use the symbol and/or logo in addition to the library's
            name)
    g. Lighting (consider safety and economy along with decor)

5. Decisions to be made:

    a. Who will be in charge of inviting bids and overseeing the job?
    b. Who will make the decisions regarding the final product and award-
            ing the contract?
    c. How will the library handle the matter regarding community impact?
            1) Run a contest for the best design
            2) Turn necessity into a newsworthy event: Invite the local news
                    media to cover the sign-putting-up ceremony
            3) Keep track of how many new patrons ask for library
                    cards in a three-month period following the
                    new sign installation--turn that into a news
                    story (see Step 44) and a sharing within the
                    profession.

6. Bidding specifications:

    a. Be certain to follow legal steps in announcing bids.
    b. Be certain everyone who bids does so on the exact same specifica-
            tions.
    c. Be certain specifications include:
            1) Insurance and Liability during installation
            2) Payment procedure
            3) Final delivery date of item(s)
            4) Closing date for accepting bids; address to where bids
                    should be sent
            5) Date, time, place of opening sealed bids
            6) Special considerations; you reserve the right to take spe-
                    cific items from several bidders--or, you want
                    the best package deal from one source

7. Keep a careful tally of bids (use the stated procedure of your board; be certain to include the points below):

NAME OF COMPANY/ PERSON	ADDRESS, TEL. #	SPECIFICATIONS/ EXCEPTIONS	ESTIMATE

PART III: SPACE

INTRODUCTION

The interior atmosphere--the placement of library furnishings and equipment--should not be an afterthought. Use of space must be well planned for librarians to function efficiently, for patrons to feel welcome and comfortable and for the professional services of the library to be promoted in a positive light.

With careful planning you can recover poorly used space. By employing a few guidelines from the decorating trade you can visually expand interior space. By using common sense you can turn an obstacle course into a free flow of traffic. Even if rebuilding or major remodeling is impossible, steps can be taken to up-date and reorganize interior space.

Before you can organize space to meet the needs of your patrons, you must know what those needs are. Refer to your previous work in Steps 7-10. Then look again at your floor plan in Step 6.

STEP 13: TAKE INVENTORY OF THE QUALITY OF SPACE USE IN YOUR LIBRARY.

YES   NO

____ ____ a.   According to your present floor plan, is there space to carry on the programs and services you and your patrons want?
____ ____ b.   Are interrelated areas close to each other?
____ ____ c.   Can patrons manuever easily in the stacks?
____ ____ d.   Is there adequate lighting in each area?
____ ____ e.   Does every person entering and leaving the library pass the circulation desk?
____ ____ f.   Is the card catalog within immediate view of patrons?
____ ____ g.   Are the walls painted institutional green?
____ ____ h.   Has anything changed since the library was remodeled in 1950?
____ ____ i.   Is there an open feeling within the library?
____ ____ j.   Are the plants doing well?
____ ____ k.   Are paintings and sculpture placed throughout the library?
____ ____ l.   Does the paint look fresh?
____ ____ m.   Is the entrance clean and uncluttered?

21

YES   NO

____ ____   n.   Are there displays throughout the library?
____ ____   o.   Is there an attractive bulletin board or display at the entrance?
____ ____   p.   Are all children's services located in one area of the building?
____ ____   q.   Do all "store front" windows have eyecatching displays?
____ ____   r.   Have you used a few vivid colors in the children's room?
____ ____   s.   Are architectural features used to their best advantage?
____ ____   t.   Are areas clearly marked?
____ ____   u.   Has low shelving been used in the children's area?
____ ____   v.   Have different textures been used throughout the library?
____ ____   w.   Is there a secure, handy place for patrons to hang wraps and place boots and umbrellas?
____ ____   x.   Is the water fountain within view?
____ ____   y.   Does your traffic pattern resemble a labyrinth? (Do you offer awards for those who make it from the entrance to the stacks and back?)
____ ____   z.   Do you provide for both continuity and change so patrons feel secure about knowing where things are and that they might find something exciting or whimsical from time to time (like a mannequin, borrowed from a local shop, intently staring at the globe, or a new cluster of chairs on display from the furniture mart or arrangements of cut flowers here and there, courtesy of the garden club....)

STEP 14: ASSESS THE INVENTORY.

1.   Make a list of the good aspects of space use in your library:

LIST OF GOOD ASPECTS	CONTRIBUTING FACTORS	CREDIT DUE TO	THANKS GIVEN

2.   Make a list of aspects that need improvements--decide on your priorities.   (You may want to finish reading this section before filling these in):

LIST OF IMPROVEMENTS NEEDED	HOW TO MAKE THEM	WHO WILL DO IT	ESTIMATED COST	TIME PLAN	JOB DONE

3.   Follow up on the lists.   Make sure things are completed.

4. Make a note of any differences the above actions make. Report to your board; share with the profession.

STEP 15: BASIC GUIDELINES FOR WORKING WITH A FLOOR PLAN.

1. Go back to Step 6. Keep your present floor plan in view.

    a. On graph paper draw a new outline of your room, complete with permanent fixtures, or use one of the copies you made during Step 6.
    b. Cut out some more patterns for furniture and equipment.

2. By manipulating the patterns you may find a way to recover poorly used space, to visually open the space you have, or to find room to add needed furnishings and equipment.

    a. Can you move the uncomfortable, tall shelving out of the children's area and replace it with low shelving to create a special area within the one large room?
    b. Will the card catalog be more accessible to patrons if its place is switched with the paperback rack that is in the front of the room?
    c. Can an area do double duty with just a little shifting of easily moved furniture?
    d. Can you provide for privacy in an open space by placing easy chairs apart from each other and by using several study carrells spaced away from each other?
    e. Where people enjoy using the library as a community center, can you arrange some furniture in groupings that permit conversations without disturbing other patrons?
    f. Can you manipulate furnishings and equipment so that there is a clear traffic pattern with ample room for people to move about and reach and use materials?
    g. Do you find that no matter what you do, there just isn't any hope? Then try bizarre things like inviting an interior design shop to come in and look you over as a public service. Or go visiting to other libraries to get ideas.
    h. Would placement at an angle be better than having everything on a north-south/east-west grid?
    i. Do you allow for a clear line of vision between office areas and patron use areas so a staff member need not always be "on the floor" to see what's going on? This is especially helpful during low-use periods when it's uneconomical to hire two staff members--one to do technical work and another to help the ocassional patron who comes in.
    j. Are you willing to get rid of furnishings and equipment that are not in good repair or that are not really used or that are simply wrong for your needs?
    k. Are you willing to put what you have to different use?

      l.   Are you using wall space as well as floor space?

     m.   Are you thinking from the patron's point of view and allowing for all sorts of individual differences?

     n.   Can you store some things for a while?

3.   Before you buy any new furniture make patterns (in scale) of the various alternatives you have narrowed your choices to and arrange them on the graph outlines of your room(s). Compare the good and bad features of each.

     a.   When selecting new furnishings, function, comfort, durability and ease of maintenance must be considered.

     b.   Chairs are preferable to sofas because they require less floor space for seating the same number of people. Chairs also provide for greater flexibility and ease in cleaning.

     c.   Check on the differences between plastic upholstered easy chairs that get ripped when children sit cross-legged while wearing buckled shoes and heat-set plastic tables and chairs that may seem too lightweight to be sturdy.

STEP 16: MAKING THE BEST USE OF THE SPACE YOU HAVE.

1.   Even when floor space is used to its best advantage, you can still stretch it visually.

     a.   A fresh coat of paint in pale yellow or light cream, a mirror, or metallic wallpaper give the illusion of small space being larger.

     b.   An area rug in a small room accentuates without reducing visual space.

     c.   Different wall treatment defines an area while maintaining an open look.

     d.   Selecting furniture in relation to the scale of the room keeps chairs and tables from becoming overpowering. A smaller scale should be used in the children's area.

     e.   Where there is a need to control light, the use of vertical blinds, one-inch louver blinds, shades or shutters will give windows a clean, uncluttered look.

     f.   Replacing worn floor coverings with carpeting not only updates the interior but lessens noise.

2.   Storage and workroom space should not be wasted when a little ingenuity will go a long way.

     a.   Install narrow shelves or peg board over tables.

     b.   Consider the addition of houseware items such as turntables to make bottles and cans more accessible in cabinets. Use drawer dividers, spice racks, hardware boxes, sack racks and stacking bins. Install pull-out shelves in under counter cabinets.

3. Dare to be different.   Put the library furniture catalog in the bottom drawer.

    a. At an auction, pick up an antique cabinet no one else wants.   Convert it into a moveable display case with glass shelves.
    b. Acquire a wicker planter but don't put plants in it--use it for books.
    c. Remove the heavy 700's from the top shelf where they inevitably get shelved and just as inevitably fall down on the heads of short people and put those same books spine-up in record bins.
    d. Never, but NEVER, put rows upon rows of books on those very lowest to the floor shelves where only contortionists can retrieve them.   Instead, convert those impossible places into fetching display areas by placing books broadside with attractive covers showing or tucking away little messages. Be creative in a dozen ways.
    e. Stop thinking "four cornered" and buy a circular display case.
    f. Bring original art into the library by creating moveable display areas.

4. Now that you have moved things around, be certain to replace your signs, unless, of course, you decided to work on this section first.

STEP 17:   ELIMINATE HAZARDS BEFORE THEY BECOME NEGATIVE PR FACTORS.

1. Look around your library for hidden hazards:

YES NO

____ ____   a. Are poinsettias and other toxic plants kept out of reach of children?
____ ____   b. Is there adequate lighting in all stairways?
____ ____   c. Can children reach banisters? (Even toddlers?)
____ ____   d. Do all glass doors have decals low enough for children to be warned and high enough for adults to take notice?
____ ____   e. Are plants and mobiles hung so that tall people can safely walk under them?
____ ____   f. Are extra-sturdy bookends holding heavy or oversized books?
____ ____   g. Are steps too steep to be easily used by children or elderly patrons?
____ ____   h. Are there places in the library (banisters, slatted dividers) or pieces of furniture (slat-back chairs, stools) where children can get head, arm, leg, foot caught?
____ ____   i. Can heavier patrons easily get through doors and stacks areas?
____ ____   j. Can people on crutches or wheelchairs easily move about the library?

YES   NO

____ ____ k. Are doors too heavy for children, elderly people or people on crutches to open?

____ ____ l. Are walkways cleared in the winter?

____ ____ m. Is there a secure place to park strollers and bicycles?

____ ____ n. Can two people, who need to do so, walk side-by-side on the sidewalks?

____ ____ o. Are book return areas well lit after hours?

____ ____ p. Are there rugs that won't lie flat?

____ ____ q. Are equipment cords and wires placed (and secured) where people won't trip and children won't play with them?

____ ____ r. Are unused outlets covered?

____ ____ s. Is equipment in good order so wires won't short or parts break off?

____ ____ t. Are there any sharp corners in the pre-school area?

____ ____ u. Is there a window directly across from the bottom stair?

____ ____ v. Are all mezzanines safe?

____ ____ w. Is there a large, absorbent mat in the entranceway so patrons do not slip on wet floors?

____ ____ x. Are exposed radiators protected with a covering and so utilized as not to require people squeezing past them?

____ ____ y. Are fire extinguishers visible, in good working order and clearly marked for use?

____ ____ z. Are fire exits marked so non-readers can find them and use them?

____ ____ aa. Are wastepaper baskets located where people can trip over them (not intentionally, of course)?

____ ____ bb. Are all free-standing objects properly weighted so that they don't fall over as people walk past them?

2. Take a looking tour. Make a note of anything that might seem like a hazard.

POSSIBLE HAZARD	LOCATION	HOW TO CHANGE	WHO WILL DO IT	JOB DONE

PART IV: DIRECT COMMUNICATIONS

INTRODUCTION

Everything <u>else</u> you do with PR can be destroyed by a letter that rubs the reader the wrong way, a notice that angers, or a tone of voice that turns a person off. The essential question of librarianship is: "How can I best interpret this library to the individual patron and to the public as a whole?" It is sometimes easier to handle "the public as a whole" than to deal with all kinds of one-to-one situations.

Direct communications can take place through a face-to-face meeting, a telephone call, a letter, or a notice. The key word is "communication," which denotes that you are listening as well as talking. The key idea is "caring," which conveys that the individual really does matter.

STEP 18: TAKE INVENTORY OF THE QUALITY OF DIRECT COMMUNICATIONS IN YOUR LIBRARY.

YES   NO

_____ _____ a. People come to your desk and say, "I'm awfully sorry to bother you, but...." or "I can see you're busy, but...."

_____ _____ b. For some reason a library letter gets returned. It is in awful shape. Maybe the less expensive stationery isn't worth the economy.

_____ _____ c. "I'm really sorry about the overdues," says a patron, "though that's an awfully cute notice."

_____ _____ d. When you pin your stationery up along with other mail you have received, you're rather proud of your choice of paper color and quality and the design of the letterhead.

_____ _____ e. You don't have a postal meter message that says something snappy about the library but you do have a rubber stamp that turns the envelope into an advertisement.

_____ _____ f. You splurged a bit and had picture postcards of your library printed. Patrons get short notes on them. They also sell well.

_____ _____ g. Sometimes days go by before the telephone rings.

YES   NO

_____ _____ h. Yesterday you had a zillion things to do but you spent the afternoon as usual talking with children who stop in after school. And, as usual, each walked out with a book, some with a title for another member of the family.

_____ _____ i. For some reason a patron got all huffy about a letter you sent him/her. But after all, it isn't his/ her library and he/she keeps asking for books that aren't even in yet. Honestly, people who watch TV talk shows are a pain.

_____ _____ j. You spend hours agonizing over how to say what you want to say in a letter but you have no trouble talking with people face-to-face.

_____ _____ k. You really dislike the impersonal computer printout message.

_____ _____ l. Vendors are always sending you things you know you didn't order, but keeping copies is such a bother you don't have anything to check against.

_____ _____ m. Four months ago you spent two days getting out a three-page personal letter to every club president. Not one has invited you to speak.

_____ _____ n. You carefully check newspapers for death notices so as not to add to the family's pain by inadvertently sending overdue notices; you wait and approach the matter in due time.

_____ _____ o. You send a regular weekly mailing to "preferred patrons," (including board members, mayor, state representatives), announcing the new books, by subject, that will be ready for circulation. This gives them a chance to be first to lay claim to readership or to get on at the top of the waiting list.

_____ _____ p. You send every new person who moves into your corporate area a personal letter inviting him/her to visit the library and to redeem the enclosed coupon for "x" items until their library card is processed.

_____ _____ q. Since that new clerk started working circulation has increased. You wonder what the secret is.

_____ _____ r. Everytime you talk with patrons you find out something new about them. This helps you connect them with materials and services in the library.

_____ _____ s. You are getting negative reaction to overdue notices. You're thinking of employing a collection agency.

_____ _____ t. Teachers seem to wait for your day off to bring students into the library. And you're the one who could tell those brats a thing or two!

_____ _____ u. You received such a nice note thanking you for the thank

YES   NO

you letter you sent to the person who conducted a library sponsored program.

____ ____ v. A vendor stopped by the other day to compliment you on the clarity of your orders. You're not sure why that's so special.

STEP 19: ASSESS THE INVENTORY.

Do you (and your staff) approach Direct Communications from the other person's point of view--that is:

> Do you write the kind of letter <u>you</u> would like to receive?
> Do you send the kind of notices that would bring a positive response from you?
> Do you analyze the needs of the other person and respond sympathetically?
> Do you feel good about yourself, your position, your library, your patrons?
> Do you recognize the attributes of a "grower" (a proprietor who keeps the business steadily moving ahead)?

1. Make a list of the good aspects of direct communications in your library:

LIST OF GOOD ASPECTS	CONTRIBUTING FACTORS	CREDIT DUE TO	THANKS GIVEN

2. Make a list of aspects that need improvement. Give them a priority rating. (You may need to complete the section before filling these points in):

LIST OF IMPROVEMENTS NEEDED	HOW TO MAKE THEM	WHO WILL DO IT	ESTIMATED COST	TIME PLAN

3. Follow up on the lists. Make sure things are completed.

4. Make a note of any differences the above actions make. Report to your board and share your ideas and successes with the profession.

STEP 20: THE LETTER

Spend the time and money required to make this seemingly unobtrusive item a major plus in your program of service.

<u>CHECKPOINTS</u>

1. Stationery

   a. Quality of paper: durability is prime (can the paper last through the mail and get to the addressee looking crisp?). You may need two kinds--one for copying machine use and one for individualized correspondence.

   b. Size: convenience counts here (can the sheet easily be filed?). The standard $8\frac{1}{2}$" x 11" is preferred. To be safe, check for postal regulations.

   c. Color: tone dictates this (go back to Part I where you assessed the style of your library; carry this through). Pure <u>white</u> is conservative; <u>tints</u> intimate warmth (most used are delicate browns, grays and blues) cream and beige are known to have "pulling power"; <u>intense colors</u>, once frowned upon, can be effective if that is part of the library's true image.

   d. Letterhead: simplicity of information and design are basic. Name, address and telephone numbers are the bare minimum; hours open, a brief identification ("Serving the people of _____ since 1853") and name of the librarian can be integrated without overloading; logo and lettering should coordinate with the image you intend to project (hire a professional to create this or run a contest with competent judges to make the choice; insist on a quality projection of image); color of ink(s) can be used to attract or harmonize --your style again dictates the choices.

205 EAST OLIVE STREET, BLOOMINGTON, ILLINOIS 61701   PHONE 309/828-6091

#2. Example of a Good Letterhead

   e. Second sheets: same quality, size and color of paper but without letterhead or other imprint.

   f. Envelopes: cost factors are dictating more widespread use of the open window in all kinds of business correspondence. In any case, the address on the envelope should be the same as the one on the inside of your letter. A return address design containing logo, name, street, city, state, zip code should be integrated with the letterhead. Weight, paper and ink color(s) and size are determined by the stationery choices. In some cases, a color contrast to the stationery can be extremely effective.

2. Content

   a. Format (or Presentation). The <u>image</u> you create will be determined by:

margins	type of complementary close
arrangement upon the page	signature
forms of punctuation	style of indentation
form for the date	choice of typeface
inside address form	quality of typing
use of titles	whether you assign a number to each
use of abbreviations	piece of correspondence and require
type of salutation	answers include that code number, too

   b. Body (or Message). Effectiveness is measured by how well the reader (addressee) is able to determine 1) why you are writing; 2) what the facts are; 3) what action needs to be taken; and how pleased he/she is to have the letter. Like all good writing, a letter needs a beginning, a middle and an ending, and it leaves the reader with a feeling of satisfaction. It is said that an effective letter writer works hard to master the ABC's--ACCURACY, BREVITY, CLARITY. Friendliness must underlie the content. Put a smile in your message, even when you are ordering pencils, and certainly when you are explaining book selection policy to a person who wants you to remove books he/she finds offensive. Never mail a letter that was written in anger or frustration. Tear it up, start over, preferably the following day. Use the word "you" in place of "I" or "we"-- "Thank you for your contribution" is better than "I appreciate the help you gave us...."

3. Perfect your skills.

   a. Flip through "How to ..." books on letter writing. Take time to go through one or more if you find you are learning something helpful.

   b. Pay attention to your reaction to letters you receive. Learn from others. Letter writing is a studied art. Analysis of the good and bad helps.

   c.   Jot down ideas that come to mind within the range of letters in a day's work at the library (are you prepared to cope with the diversity?):

      1) orders to vendors
      2) replies to questions
      3) invitation to a speaker
      4) support of legislation to an elected official
      5) suggestion for legislation to an elected official
      6) thank you to a donor
      7) special recognition in honor of ...
      8) reply to an unhappy citizen
      9) reply to a happy citizen (!)
     10) cover letter with a grant proposal
     11) request for a place on the agenda of the corporate authority meeting
     12) request for free materials
     13) letter to the editor
     14) condolences

STEP 21: THE NOTICE.

If you want the addressee to pay attention to the message you will have to make the notice attention-getting.

CHECKPOINTS

1. Form

   a.   The unusual or the unexpected is to receive a notice that is attractive, friendly, humorous, sympathetic and well-designed, within the bounds of what people in your community accept (getting too cute may offend some while it is right on target for others).

   b.   Call attention to the notice in two ways--run a contest "To design the kind of overdue notice you wouldn't mind receiving" and publicize the responses you get.

   c.   No matter what the reason for the notice (ordered book arrived, overdue, special meeting, etc.) the postcard can be the easiest way to communicate. Print a variety on card stock of various colors with a preprinted message or with space to personalize.

   d.   Investigate the form of notices that you receive. Borrow ideas that seem to work.

   e.   If you send computer printouts, personalize the message along with the facts.

2. Content

    a. Instead of cold, curt efficiency, send a notice that reads like a conversation:

> HI!
>
> DID YOU GET BUSY AND OVERLOOK THE DUE DATE ON YOUR LIBRARY BOOK? WELL, JUST DROP IT BY THE LIBRARY ANY MONDAY-SATURDAY DURING THE HOURS LISTED ABOVE. OTHERWISE, USE THE BOOKDROP. WHILE YOU'RE HERE YOU MIGHT WANT TO CHECK OUT SOMETHING ELSE OF INTEREST TO YOU.
>
> SEE YOU SOON,
>
> XXXXXXXXXX
> LIBRARIAN
>
> HI!
>
> DO YOU STILL NEED THE BOOK YOU BORROWED? COME IN MONDAY-SATURDAY DURING THE HOURS LISTED ABOVE (OR CALL -) TO RENEW IT. YOU MIGHT ALSO FIND SOME OTHER MATERIAL ON THE SAME TOPIC THAT YOU WOULD LIKE TO BORROW.
>
> LOOKING FORWARD TO SEEING YOU!
>
> BEST WISHES,
>
> XXXXXXXXXX
> LIBRARIAN
>
> HI!
>
> YOU HAVE A BOOK SOMEONE ELSE WANTS. PLEASE RETURN IT DIRECTLY TO THE LIBRARY MONDAY-SATURDAY DURING THE HOURS ABOVE OR DROP IT IN THE BOOK RETURN. IF YOU STILL NEED DATA ON THAT PARTICULAR TOPIC, LET US HELP YOU FIND OTHER MATERIAL THAT IS EQUALLY INTER-ESTING TO YOU.
>
> LOOKING FORWARD TO SEEING YOU!
>
> BEST WISHES,
>
> XXXXXXXXXX
> LIBRARIAN

HI!

THE MATERIAL SPECIALLY ORDERED FOR YOU IS IN. PLEASE DROP BY THE LIBRARY MONDAY-SATURDAY DURING THE HOURS LISTED ABOVE AND ASK TO SEE _____ OR _____.
THEY HAVE YOUR MATERIAL PACKAGED AND READY TO BE CHECKED OUT.

LOOKING FORWARD TO SEEING YOU!

XXXXXXXXXXX
LIBRARIAN

b. Experiment with different approaches. Keep a tally so you can determine what works best with each particular group.

STEP 22: THE TELEPHONE.

Develop the kind of telephone personality that projects warmth along with efficiency in a natural flow of conversation.

CHECKPOINTS

1. Salutation

a. Immediate identification of the institution is essential. A nice twist is: "Thank you for calling XTown Library" or "XTown Library, how may I help you?" or "XTown Library, Mrs. Tree speaking."

b. Tone of voice makes the difference. You may have to resort to the tape recorder to tell you how you rate: friendly, cold, irritable, pushed, at loose ends, vague.

c. What you do to the ending of words causes a reaction. If your voice goes up at the end of words you may leave the caller perplexed. (Say "hello," raising the pitch on the "lo." It seems as if you are asking rather than answering.)

d. Support of the voice determines firmness, breathiness, temerity. While shouting isn't necessary, neither is the opposite. (Say "XTown Library" taking short pants of breath all the way through. The disjointedness is annoying.) Even if you hurried to catch the call on the fifth ring, stop to catch your breath. Sultriness can be nice for late-night weather reports, but it might turn off a caller to the library to hear a purring greeting--"Eehhhxtownnnnn li-uh-brah-eh-reee."

2. Determine exactly what the caller needs.

a. Paying full attention to what is being said means total concentration despite distractions. Have a pad and pencil available at all times. Learn to pick out the key elements in the conversation. This takes practice and training and is akin to conducting a good reference interview.

b. Satisfying the caller's needs either immediately or by follow-up is a measure of the efficiency of the operation. If you don't know the answer or don't have the material, say so and try to be positive about how you or the caller can get the answer. Never say, "That is an inappropriate request for the library" or "We don't accept crank questions" or "This is the library, not the train station...." Instead, say: "Thank you for calling the library. May I suggest that you call Legal Aid at _____ or your personal lawyer to receive a satisfactory answer to your question." OR "Thank you for calling the library, but we don't have Prince Albert in a can. We do however, have a lot of good books on humor. Why not stop by and look us over?" OR "Thank you for calling the library. The train schedule we have here may not be the best source for the information you need. May I suggest that you call _____." THIS MEANS THAT THE LIBRARY NEEDS TO HAVE A HANDY, EFFICIENT INFORMATION SOURCE WITHIN TELEPHONE REACH. TO DEVELOP SUCH A RESOURCE TAKES TIME BUT THE RESULTS CAN BE WORTHWHILE.

c. Keep a running tally of the kinds of transactions generated by a telephone call to the library. Develop a tally sheet:

Date	Time	Name of Caller	Reason for Calling	How Satisfied	Staff Mem.

3. Ending the telephone call

a. Always thank the caller for calling. Leave the impression that you welcome hearing from him/her.

b. Be sure that the caller is fully satisfied or comprehends what action he/she is to take--"We will order these books through Interlibrary Loan. You will receive a note (or a telephone call) when the materials arrive. Do you know our hours?" or "We will mail you an application for Talking Book Service. Please follow the directions on the application form. We would be delighted to have you come by the library but if it is not convenient everything can be handled by mail."

STEP 23: THE FACE-TO-FACE CONVERSATION.

Your clerical and managerial duties are secondary to your personal contact with the library public.

CHECKPOINTS

1. The attitude you project
   a. Are you the essence of "Don't bother me, I'm shelving...."
   b. Do you look available without being pushy?
   c. Are you easily identified as a library staff member? (See p. 103, "Name tags")
   d. Do you know where to find things and can you easily direct people to their location?

2. Determining exactly what the patron needs
   a. Listen and restate the request, if necessary.
   b. Neither overwhelm (push the latest Washington exposé on the person who merely wants the address of his/her U.S. Representative) nor overlook a source (forget to mention the audio-text cassettes along with books and films on how to set up a small business).

3. Ending the contact
   a. Be genuinely happy to have talked with the patron. Never give service grudgingly. <u>Never</u> say, "Well now that you have what you need I can get back to work...." You have been working!
   b. Be sure the patron knows how to use the materials you suggested and is aware of due dates and how to return the materials.

4. Keep a record of transactions

STEP 24: PERSONAL CONTACT-POINTS OF HIGH SENSITIVITY.

1. Registration: Whoever handles registration of new patrons or registration into a library program may well establish the service image for the entire library.

   a. What is the registration form? Does it ask questions that are offensive (list husband's name, if a female applicant, but male applicants need not list name of wife)? Does it ask questions that are irrelevant (do you use alcoholic beverages or smoke)? Is the form attractive or a ditto sheet with strikeovers and weak imprint? Can the form easily be filed and processed? Have you thought about it as a PR factor?

   b. What is the attitude of the registration librarian (or clerk)? Is this person trained for the position? Is this person familiar with all aspects of the library operation so that questions can be answered with intelligence and assurance? Is this individual a good "people person"?

   c. What materials do you have on hand to introduce the new patron to the library, its materials, services and importance in the life of the individual and community?

d. Is there an immediate contact with a library staff member so that the new patron has a friend? Why not print up a business card with the library's name, address, hours, telephone number and name of an individual contact on the staff and give this to the new patron? He/she can use this as a point of reference just as he/she would in a store.

e. Is there a tour of the library available for every new patron? It can be a guided tour or a self-help one with an appropriate brochure or a brochure and cassette tape with player (let's borrow a gimmick from museums).

f. How long is it before a person receives a library card? Is there immediate access (even if the amount of materials that may be borrowed is limited)?

2. Reference: Very few people like to admit that there is something they need to know. Thus, the reference librarian must be a gentleperson and a scholar!

a. How good is your reference service? If the librarian is asked a question can a correct answer be obtained? If the patron wants to locate data on his/her own, are the reference tools readily available? Do you keep a card file of questions so that you can refer to it (often the same question gets asked again)?

b. How effective is the reference librarian? Finding data and communicating it are two different skills. Does the reference librarian make a habit of saying, "Really, this was a terribly simple question--a fourth grader could have found the answer ..."? Does someone on the library staff take the trouble to show people how to use reference tools? (Many people are bewildered by the card catalog and the Readers' Guide ...)

c. How accessible is your library's reference area? Is it clearly marked where patrons may use materials? (Having reference data in the director's office is not the best idea.) Does your placement and filing of materials make sense to others? (Who else would think to look for flower garden tips under "Lovely" in the vertical file?) Is there adequate lighting and work space? Are there written instructions (in everyday English) for the patrons who like to help themselves (reminders like, "LOOK IN THE FILM CATALOG UNDER STORYTELLING," along with books on the topic)?

3. Check-out: If overdues, theft, and loss are prevalent in your library, perhaps your check-out procedure does not generate a positive attitude.

a. Do you give patrons a chance to reverse poor judgment with a nicely designed reminder near the door: HAVE YOU REMEMBERED TO CHECK OUT ALL LIBRARY MATERIALS BEFORE PASSING

THROUGH THE ELECTRONIC INSPECTION DEVICE? THE DESK IS
TO YOUR RIGHT.

b.   Does the check-out librarian say, "This book is checked out until
the xth of Nth.   To renew it you will have to bring the book back
to the library" (or whatever your procedure is).   A useful gimmick
could be to insert a dated bookmark with each book.   (See illustration no. 3.)

GUESS
WHAT TIME
IT IS.

3.   Dated Bookmark

c.   Does it take a long time for people to get checked out? Review
your circulation procedure to speed it up.   A patron who feels mis-
treated will not follow due dates happily.

d. Is the check-out procedure a pleasant, positive experience so that people feel good about the library and its service and have no interest in "ripping it off"?

4. Perfecting skills

Take an inventory of these three departments. What is their PR rating? What steps can you take to improve? What good points do you have that you could share within the profession?

STEP 25: ADJUNCTS TO DIRECT COMMUNICATION.

1. The Postal Meter Message
   a. Work out a message that is in keeping with your image and work with the postal meter representative to incorporate it into the postal meter.
   b. Use words and a symbol or either alone.
   c. To get ideas, begin reading your envelopes.

2. The Rubber Stamp
   a. Develop a variety of messages and symbols and use any number of ink pad colors. Stamp away at whim.
   b. Check with local printers or office supply outlets or order your rubber stamps via catalogs. Some ready-made products can also be used along with your custom designs.
   c. Create a design that will stamp clearly, be easily readable and carry a universal message.

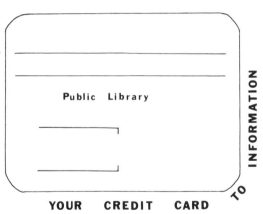

4. Example of a Rubber Stamp or Postal Meter Message

3. The Picture Postcard
   a. Work with professional photographers, artists and printers for both the picture and the message. (Check the yellow pages for companies specializing in producing picture postcards.)
   b. Consider the cost per unit for the total operation when ordering quantity. It is usually more economical to print more and retail the excess amount of what you actually need for library business.
   c. Choose picture(s) and copy that show the library to its best advantage.

PART V: BUILDING SKILLS FOR
VISUAL PR ACTIVITIES

"It now takes me twice as long to go through my junk mail and adver-tisements! Before the PR workshops I threw things out. Now I'm finding plenty of ideas and pictures and captions I can use."

"These dry transfer letters <u>are</u> easy to use. They make everything I put together look so professional."

"I can't believe I'm making bookmarks that everyone likes!"

"People smile when they see my posters. I can't tell you how good that makes me feel."

STEP 26: GENERAL STEPS TO ORGANIZE YOUR WORK.

1. Decide on the purpose of the visual PR material: To introduce a new service for young people and initiate action for them to use it.

2. Choose a theme: "Dial-A-Story" -- call from your own home.

3. Write down and verify all of the information that must go into the mes-sage:
<u>What</u>--Dial-A-Story   <u>Who</u>--anyone, but especially the very
<u>Where</u>--987-1234   young
<u>When</u>--anytime--24 hours a day   <u>Why</u>--because it's fun
                                       <u>How</u>--dial correctly, listen, hang up

4. Decide on the method of distribution:
    a. Mail to everyone through telephone bills--arrange with telephone company.
    b. Distribute through nursery and kindergarten-2nd grade classes.
    c. Distribute to patrons checking out materials in library.
    d. Distribute through pediatrician offices and child care clinics.

5. Decide on the form of ink-print material and the size appropriate for distribution: Bookmark on cardstock cut to fit into envelopes for mailing.

6. Decide on the number needed: Mailing plus 1000 for general distribu-tion = 3500.

7. List all of the pictorial elements that can symbolize your theme and message. You need only one or two "central figures"--attention getting devices. Other parts--elements--must be keyed to the central figures:
    a. Telephone
    b. Child dialing telephone
    c. Child listening, receiver to ear
    d. Child holding book while holding telephone
    After discussion with staff and a sampling of parents and young children you settle on a posed photo of a child listening to telephone. You take (or get) the photo, have the release for use without pay signed and develop it to the size you need for the paste-up)

8. Decide on the caption--attention-getting message:

    DIAL-A-STORY

    987-1234

    (Under that, the copy will read:)
    A 3-minute taped story or poem available 24 hours daily as a service of Xtown Public Library

9. Make sketches of how the item can look. Think about each element of the design--art (drawings, photos); lettering; copy (the print message). Experiment with different arrangements, keeping the design simple and uncluttered. Try several designs out (market test*) on a sample of the

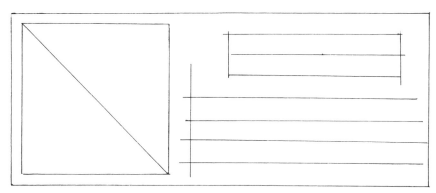

5. Layout of Dial-A-Story
    Bookmark

audience you are targeting the item to. Listen to what they say and make adjustments.

---

*It is presumed that you will have chosen a duplicating method, a printer and have worked out your budget before going into the market testing. Keep a file of costs per item on hand so that you can target into the best duplicating method. You will also want other materials, such as posters and handouts, as well as media publicity for the example we used here. This is just one phase.

10. Decide on the colors (based on market testing)
    (Black ink on white cardstock)

11. Decide on the style of lettering (based on market testing)
    (Block lettering representative of what a young child creates)

12. Transfer the final design to the paper or posterboard of the weight
    that is best for the purpose. (Cardstock sturdy enough to hold the
    various elements.)

13. Complete the item you are making by adding or pasting down each part.
    (Photo pasted in area marked for it. Block lettering inked-in on the
    guidelines and guide-lettering done in blue pencil. Typed copy pasted
    in space marked for it.)

STEP 27: MATERIALS TO HAVE ON HAND.

1. For measuring and drawing guide-lines:
   a. Ruler   d. Right-angle triangle
   b. Yardstick   e. Compass
   c. T-Square

2. For marking and drawing:
   a. Pencils: blue, for non-copying lines and sketches; #2, soft lead;
      #3, hard lead
   b. Pens: felt tip of various widths; specialized lettering and drawing
      pens
   c. Magic markers
   d. Crayons
   e. Water colors and washes
   f. Poster paints, brushes
   g. Inks of various colors

3. For cutting:
   a. Paper cutter   e. Hole punch
   b. Shears of various lengths f. Utility knife
   c. Scissors   g. Razor blade in case
   d. Pinking shears   h. Wire cutter

4. For correcting:
   a. Soft eraser
   b. Liquid paper
   c. Rubber cement pick-up

5. For attaching:
   a. Thumb tacks   g. Spring clothespins
   b. Push pins   h. String and yarn
   c. Straight pins   i. Double sticking tape
   d. Stapler, staplegun   j. Masking tape
   e. Glue   k. Non-glare transparent tape
   f. Rubber cement   l. Wire

6. For drawing on:
   a. Mimeobond white paper
   b. Cardboard
   c. Poster (Railroad) board of various weights, colors, sizes
   d. Sketching paper
   e. Graph paper of various line differences
   f. Butcher paper

7. For background:
   a. Fadeless paper
   b. Textured paper
   c. Fabrics
   d. Doilies
   e. Wallpaper (samples)
   f. Wrapping paper
   g. Scraps of fabric
   h. Flannel
   i. Felt
   j. Burlap
   k. Paneling
   l. Carpeting

8. For 3-dimensional effects:
   a. Cotton batting
   b. Netting
   c. Ribbon
   d. Book jackets
   e. Items of clothing
   f. Real items

9. For lettering:
   a. Dry-transfer
   b. Vinyl peel-off
   c. Stencils
   d. Pin back
   e. Alphabet stamps & stamp pad

10. For preserving:
    a. Acetate sheets
    b. Clear contact paper
    c. Frames (glass)
    d. Filing cabinets

11. For hanging on:
    a. Peg board
    b. Plaster board
    c. Cork board
    d. Burlap
    e. Racks
    f. Clothes line
    g. Dowel rods

12. For getting ideas from:
    a. Coloring books
    b. Junk mail
    c. Newspapers, magazines
    d. Catalogs
    e. Advertisements from other sources
    f. How-to books

13. For general use:
    a. Saw
    b. Claw hammer
    c. Tack hammer
    d. Nails of various sizes
    e. Screw drivers
    f. Screws
    g. Hinges
    h. Wire
    i. Plywood
    j. Butcher paper
    k. Newsprint
    l. Paper of various kinds

14. For special effects:
    a. Spotlights
    b. Pipe cleaners
    c. Clothes hangers
    d. Boxes of various sizes
    e. Cameras (black & white for photos in newsletters, etc.; color slides for shows)

15. For art:
   a. Book jackets
   b. Clip art (purchased, non-copyright art sold expressly to be used for creating posters, brochures, bookmarks, etc.)
   c. Photographs
   d. Color book drawings
   e. Original drawings
   f. Children's art
   g. Greeting cards
   h. Commercially produced lines and borders

STEP 28: FIND IDEAS AND MAKE THEM YOUR OWN.

1. Look at all sorts of printed material. Ask the question: "Can I use this to create a library flier, display, poster, bookmark, etc.?"

   a. Save things--ads, greeting cards, book jackets, magazines, junk mail, newspaper headlines, PR materials from other libraries, etc.

   b. Make notes on ideas you find in books and local business publicity and advertising.

   c. When you find an idea you like SAVE IT. File by seasonal ideas, topics, items (bookmarks, posters, etc.)

2. How to use the items you collect:

   a. Look at the format of an ad in a magazine or newspaper, a mailer, a bookmark, etc.
      1) Can the layout serve as a guide for your next flier, bookmark, etc.?
      2) Can you add or change words to make it a library caption? ("HOORAY FOR HOLLYWOOD" ... "HOORAY FOR BOOKS" ... "BRAVO FOR BOOKS" ...)
      3) Can the lettering be cut out and used on paste-ups or serve as a guide for hand-lettering? Ornate lettering can be cut out and used as first letters. Whole words can be used as attention-getting headlines. Check at local art supply shops for dry transfer lettering in that style.
      4) Can the artwork be used for one-of-a-kind posters? If it is not copyrighted art you can clip it and use it. If you like the effect of a photo find a photo to use in your next brochure.
      5) Can you repeat a striking color combination?
      6) Is the flier from Ytown Library on paper you like? Find out from them where they order their paper or take the sample around to supply shops in your area and ask that it be ordered for you.

    b. Adapt the various elements to use in any item you need to create.

STEP 29: LAYOUT ARRANGEMENTS.

1. Experiment with shapes to get a balanced, attractive arrangement of the various elements (Headline or caption, art, copy).
CUT OUT FOUR RECTANGLES: one 3"x1"; two 1½"x2"; one 5"x2"

    a. Formal Arrangement is symmetrical. One side mirrors the opposite. See illustration no. 6 opposite. Create different symmetrical arrangements with the four rectangles.

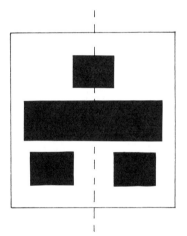

6. Formal Arrangement

    b. Informal Arrangement is asymmetrical. Each half is different, but the arrangement as a whole is harmonious. See illustration no. 7.

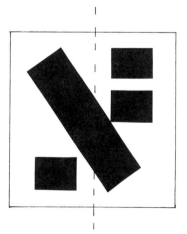

7. Informal Arrangement

    c. Experiment with many different layouts using circles, triangles and squares that you cut out. Be sure that the elements are related to each other and are pleasing to the eye.

2. Basic Layout Arrangements. See illustrations 8-14 below.

8. Step
Arrangement

9. Pyramid
Arrangement

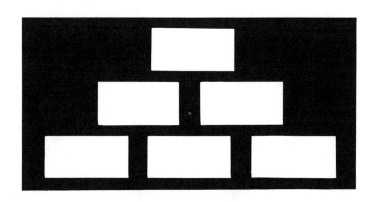

10. Fan
Arrangement

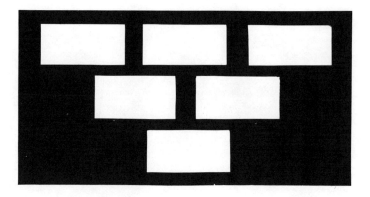

11. Zig Zag
Arrangement

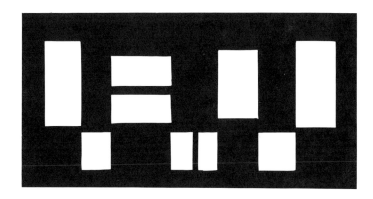

12. Landscape
Arrangement

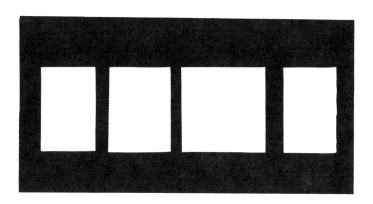

13. Repetitive
Panels

14. Magazine
Arrangement

3. Focal Point: Have one point which attracts the viewer's attention. Color, lettering, white space, photograph, etc. can be combined to attract the viewer to that one point.

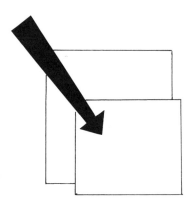

15. Focal Point

STEP 30: TECHNIQUES.

1. <u>Paste-up</u>. Paste-up art is used for creating a master for duplication (office copier, speed printing, offset printing).

   a. Prepare each element separately--the headline or caption, the art, the copy.
   b. Arrange the design on paper cut to the finished size. It must be white paper.
   c. View it critically--does it look good, does it attract and hold attention?
   d. Make changes, if necessary.

e. Mark the finished arrangement with <u>light</u> gudielines on the final piece of paper.
f. Rubber cement each part in place (See #2 below.)
g. Remove any excess adhesive that shows around the edges. Use a rubber cement "pick-up" or a bit of dried rubber cement rolled into a ball.
h. Remove dirt smudges and marks that may reproduce.
i. If excess marks don't erase, white them out with typewriter correction paint carefully applied.
j. Blacken faded-out places with a black felt-tip pen.
k. Gaps that may reproduce as unwanted lines can be covered with white correction paint.
l. Use commercially produced lines and borders for clean, straight lines (visit art supply stores).

2. <u>Rubber Cement</u>. Rubber cement provides neat, wrinkle-free pasting for every kind of art work.

   a. After marking where each piece will go on the paper, turn each piece over and apply rubber cement to the entire area. Let the rubber cement dry. Lay these pieces on clean scratch paper during this process.
   b. Rubber cement the marked areas (on the final paper) where each piece will be adhered.
   c. When both are dry, place a sheet of tracing (onion skin) paper between them and position the "cut out."
   d. Pulling from the top, slowly remove the tracing paper and smooth the cut out down as contact is made with the rubber cement on the paper. In this way, the cut out is positioned without worrying about getting it stuck in the wrong place.
   e. Remove any excess adhesive.

3. <u>Graphite Tracing</u>. Used to transfer your own art work to the finished product when paste-up is not a good solution.

   a. Blacken the backside of the art work with a soft graphite pencil.
   b. Place the back side of the art work with a soft graphite pencil. on the paper where the final art product will appear.
   c. Trace your art work with a very hard pencil (#3). The blackened graphite acts as a carbon for tracing.
   d. Remove the blackened art work.
   e. Finish the final art work.

4. <u>Enlarging a pattern</u> (Decreasing a pattern). Used to make an item smaller or larger, keeping the same proportions.

   a. Use graph paper that you can see through or draw a rectangle and a grid of equally spaced squares over the original, as shown in illustration no. 16 on page 50.
   b. Draw another larger rectangle, the size you want the art work to be. Divide it into equally spaced squares that are larger than those of

the original but that are equal in number to those in the smaller rectangle. (If there are 6 vertical squares in the small rectangle, there must be 6 vertical squares in the larger rectangle.)

c. Draw in each of the larger squares the part of the pattern that is in the corresponding smaller square.

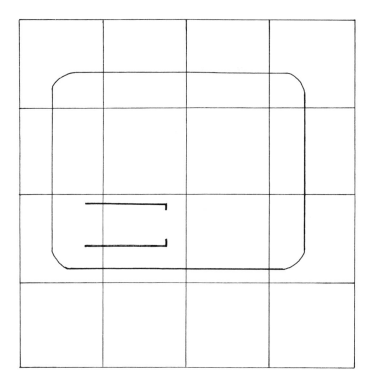

16. Enlarging a Pattern

5. Lettering. Used in paste-up, posters, signs when typewriter type is not sufficient.

a. Lettering options:

1) Dry transfer
2) Hand lettering
3) Stencil
4) Peel-off plastic
5) Rubber stamp letters
6) Cut-out letters
7) Machine lettering (small presses, dry transfer by machine
8) Gimmicks (string writing, toothpicks glued down, etc.)

b. Draw light guidelines with a T-square or a right-angle triangle
    1) Make sure all corners of the poster board or paper are square. Place the triangle over the corner of the board or paper. If edges are covered by the triangle, the board is square.

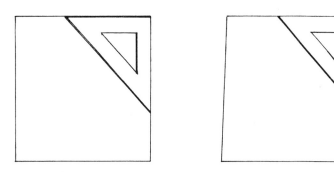

Square   Not Square

17. Square Edge

2) Measure from the top the distance at which you want your first line of lettering to be placed.
3) Make a small pencil mark at this point.
4) Draw marks at the correct distances apart to accommodate the size of lettering you are using.
5) Use a T-square to make horizontal lines. Place the T-square edge against the left edge of the poster board or paper. (The long edge is placed on the mark and is parallel with the bottom edge of the board or paper.)

Draw a line, using a soft pencil-lead. Repeat for as many lines as you need.

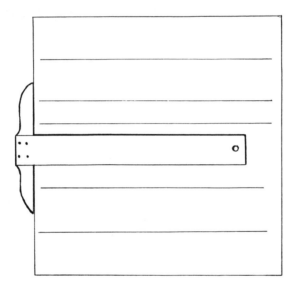

18. Marking Distances and
    Drawing Guidelines with
    a T-Square

If you use a right-angle triangle to draw guidelines place one leg of the triangle smack against the edge of the board. The second edge is placed on the mark and is parallel with the bottom edge.

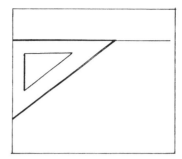

19. Drawing Guidelines with a Right-Angle Triangle

c. Dry transfer lettering is available in art supply stores and should come with instructions. The process takes a little getting used to in order to get the spacing between letters just right--not too close together, not too far apart and even throughout.

    1) Draw a light pencil line under the space where the lettering is to appear. (Use a blue pencil for paste-up. This eliminates having to erase the line.)

    2) Place the letter, with the sheet positioned for its guidelines, over the space on the paper where you want the letter to appear.

    3) Rub a blunt pencil point (or a store-bought wooden stylus) over the specific letter, to transfer that letter from the clear plastic to the paper. Take care not to smudge other letters in the process.

    4) Repeat the process for the remaining letters.

    5) Erase (gently!) the pencil line between the letters.

d. Hand lettering can be fun and practical if you are willing to be inventive. See illustration no. 20 for examples.

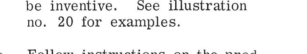

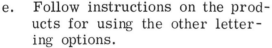

e. Follow instructions on the products for using the other lettering options.

20. Hand Lettering Options

6. <u>Mounting</u>. This technique involves placing art work on a background that enhances the art work.

    a. Experiment with placing the art work on backgrounds with narrow and wide borders. What brings out the art work best?

    b. Experiment with various colors. A red background color will bring out all the reds in a piece of art work.

    c. Always use fadeless paper for background.

    d. For vertical illustrations make the bottom margin the widest and the top margin wider than the side margins.

    e. For horizontal illustrations the top margin should be narrower than the side margins and again the bottom margin should be the widest. See illustration **21** opposite.

    f. Use double mounting to bring in two colors or two textures. The proportions for margins on the bottom background should remain as for "d" and "e" above.

    g. Use the rubber cement technique for adhering art work to background.

    h. Striking effects can be achieved by using materials other than paper or poster-board for background. Experiment with fabric, carpeting, wood, placemats, etc.

21. Margins for Mounting

    i. When creating bulletin boards, you can staple, pin or tack art to background materials.

7. <u>Positive-Negative</u>. This technique creates a dramatic effect with very little effort.

a. Work with a simple design--the basic shapes (square, rectangle, circle, triangle), easily recognized silhouettes (butterfly, heart, diamond, clover-leaf, sail boat) or dramatic landscapes (mountain peaks, corn husks at harvest, city buildings).

b. Use two colors of contrasting paper--one dark, one light.

c. One sheet of paper is twice the size, in the same proportions, as the other. See illustration 22 below.

d. Fold the smaller sheet in half.

e. Sketch the design on the folded paper, with the center of the design on the fold of the paper.

f. Using sharp shears, cut out the design with the paper still folded. See illustration 23 below.

g. Unfold the cut-out and the sheet.

h. Lay the cut-out on one half of the larger piece of paper and the outline on the opposite half. See illustration 24 below.

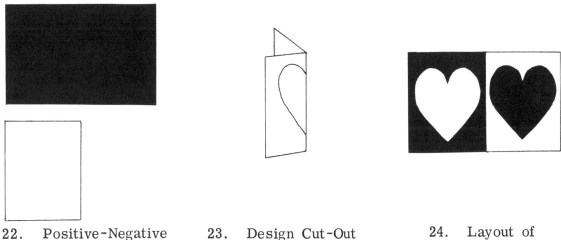

22. Positive-Negative   23. Design Cut-Out   24. Layout of
     Paper in Two   for Positive-   Positive-
     Sizes   Negative   Negative

i. Adhere the parts with the rubber cement technique.

j. Use this as a background for posters, bulletin boards, paste-ups for brochures, fliers, bookmarks, etc. Adhere messages for the best effect.

STEP 31: APPROACHES. (Various ways to put together visual PR materials)

1. Realistic manner: Photograph or a drawing that is almost like a photograph.

2. Stylized: A conventional pattern that is not realistic, yet you recognize the item.

3. Symbolic: Using a symbol that people associate with the topic or idea--library: book.

4. Abstract: Not a recognizable thing, instead a non-representational design.

5. Homespun: Giving the material a cozy, handcrafted look.

6. Humorous: Handle the topic in a light, fun manner--Woodstock building a roof over his nest to protect the library books he borrowed.

7. Pop: Using items that are popular or current--superheroes announcing a program.

8. Formal: Engraved invitation to a gala event at the library.

9. Historical: Pulling a distinctive look of a period and using it for your own purposes--art nouveau, art deco, Victorian, Roaring 20's (flapper).

10. Holiday: Realistic, stylized, symbolic or abstract items--Santa Claus; Easter bunny; flag, drum, fife; turkey & Pilgrim.

11. Seasonal: Colors or items associated with seasons--fall=browns, oranges, golds; spring=pastels, tulips, rabbits; summer=blues, greens, bright yellow; winter=white, grey, bare trees. Avoid stereotypes, as a librarian with a bun hairdo, sour expression.

STEP 32: STEPS IN MAKING A SIGN.

Signs are lettered notices which give directions, information or announcements. A good sign is made neatly on sturdy boards with clear lettering appropriate for the use. (See also PART VI for a discussion on the uses of signs.)

1. Decide on the message
   a. Stress the positive.
   b. Gather all of the data to be included in the sign. Double-check for accuracy.
   c. Be brief.
   d. Try out the message on someone else to check on its clarity.

2. Decide on the placement of the finished sign
   a. A sign to be seen from a distance needs large lettering.
   b. The lettering on a table-top sign can be of moderate size.
   c. A hanging sign requires different materials from a self-standing sign, etc.

3. Decide on the style and size of lettering
   a. Directional signs in the same area should use the same style of lettering and same color poster board.
   b. Information or announcement signs should stay with the same family of lettering. Introduce variety by using differing sizes within this family.
   c. A unique blending of typefaces can be attractive. This takes skill.

4. Decide on the design of the sign
   a. Do some practicing and trial runs before making a final sketch.
   b. Be attentive to legibility and eye-appeal.

5. Draw guidelines, ALWAYS, even when you become an expert sign-maker!
   a. Measure off distances and follow the steps under "b" of "Lettering" on page 51.
   b. The "old bulletin board trick" is to attach a string between two pushpins or tacks and to attach the letters along the string line. When done, remove the string.

6. Preserve the finished sign with a clear adhesive paper if the sign will be used for a period of time.

7. Store seasonal (or once-in-awhile) signs in a flat, well-marked area so that you have both durability and accessibility.

STEP 33: STEPS IN MAKING POSTERS. (Signs with something added)

1. Uses
   a. To announce an upcoming event.
   b. To give specific or general information.

2. General tips
   a. A poster must first stop the viewer and completely hold his/her attention so that the viewer is willing to read and note and act on the information.
   b. Use only non-fade materials.
   c. For one-of-a-kind posters additional interest can be added with texture, 3-dimensional objects, original art work that can't be duplicated, copyright cut-outs from magazines or newspapers or other ads.
   d. Pockets can be added for the distribution of fliers, bookmarks, etc.
   e. Make the major word or words LARGE and eyecatching.
   f. Don't crowd lettering.
   g. Use one, or at the most two, styles of lettering. Gain variety by

       using different sizes of the same lettering family.

h.   To use the poster over an extended period of time or to store and use it again, cover it with clear contact paper.

i.   Hang and store as you would a sign.

j.   Use any one of the numerous 'how to' books on poster making to get ideas.

k.   Collect caption ideas from various sources.

l.   Look at all kinds of posters to see what makes each good or poor.

3.   <u>How to Make Posters</u>
   Follow STEPS 26-32.

PART VI: SIGNS

STEP 34: SIGNS SEEN FROM THE OUTSIDE IN.

1. Uses of signs
    a. Giving library hours
    b. Special instructions (book drop, deliveries, holiday closings)
    c. Directions (parking in rear, ring for assistance in opening door)

2. General rules to follow
    a. The sign should be legible through glass
    b. The message must be short, specific, clear
    c. Use durable materials
    d. Use non-fade colors and materials
    e. Create a design in keeping with the style of the building
    f. Place the sign where it can be seen by everyone (children and adults)

3. How to make signs
    a. State the message. Double-check it. Have someone else check. Have you left something out? Have you put too much in? Is each word spelled correctly? Are days and dates correct?
    b. Gather the materials
        1) A sturdy board, cut to size and in the right color
        2) A yardstick or ruler (whichever is the right size for your sign)
        3) A sharpened pencil (soft or blue lead for easy erasing)
        4) A clean eraser
        5) Lettering that is right for your style and purpose
        6) Some way of hanging or affixing the sign
        7) Transparent (clear) contact paper to preserve the sign
    c. Make the sign (follow techniques on pages 56-57, PART V)
    d. Hang the sign
    e. When necessary, store for re-use in a dry, flat place that is label-ed for easy access.

STEP 35: SIGNS PLACED INSIDE THE LIBRARY.

1. Uses of signs
    a. For general instructions:
        1) How to obtain a library card
        2) How to check out materials

59

      3) How to become a friend of the library
      4) How to sign up for a story program
      5) How to order interlibrary loan materials
      6) How to get films, tapes, recordings from the central desk area

  b. For orientation to the physical layout:
      1) A floor plan with a notation "You are here" for the whole building
      2) A floor plan for a specific section of the building

  c. For identification of areas:
      1) Offices (Director, Technical Services ...)
      2) Service areas (Circulation Desk, Registration, A-V Equipment)
      3) Patron use areas (Browsing, Young Adults Collection, Puppet Stage)

  d. Identifying materials on shelves:
      1) Dewey Decimal or Library of Congress designations
      2) Standard items by subject (Self Help, Large Print, Antiques)
      3) Bold "ABC" designations for separation by authors, as for fiction and picture books

  e. For use in displays and exhibits:
      Enhance a good display with neat, legible identification signs.

  f. "Labeling" library staff members:
      Name tags are mobile advertisements and a source of identification. A well-designed, durable name tag gives a staff member a feeling of being an important part of the operation. A staff attitude of service, efficiency and friendliness promotes a positive atmosphere for the patron. (The library should let staff members know that their name tags will be presented to them upon completion of their service because during their tenure they made a difference.) Provide a name tag that is a quality product and that projects a high degree of professionalism.

2. General rules to follow
  a. Choose one style of lettering for each category of signs.
  b. Place signs where they can be seen by tall or short people.
  c. Develop graphics for pre-literate patrons (three-year-olds use the library but can't read lettered signs).
  d. Consider safety in the placement of signs.
  e. Avoid free-hand lettering unless you are an expert calligrapher.
  f. Whenever possible, integrate your logo and library name into the design of the sign.

3. Signs commercially produced according to your specifications or purchased from a catalog stock
  a. Library materials companies (check advertising that comes direct, visit booths at library conferences, ask librarians when you visit other libraries where they got their signs).
  b. Letterpress printers (check the yellow pages under "printers").
  c. Commercial artists (check the yellow pages under "advertising").
  d. Scout other public buildings to find out who did their signs.

4. Sign-making equipment you buy (check catalogs and local stores)
   a. Slotted, changeable message boards
   b. Sign-maker kits
   c. Pinback letters and numbers for cork or other soft backgrounds

5. Signs you create
   a. One-of-a-kind signs. You can take certain liberties with make-it-yourself-signs: cut pictures, slogans, ads, headlines (anything) out of magazines and newspapers and adapt them to your needs. EXAMPLE: A series of photographs advertising symphonies on TV were adapted with the tag-line "WE CONDUCT OUR BUSINESS WITH AS MUCH SENSITIVITY" and "ANYONE WHO KNOWS THE SCORE READS--MUSIC BOOKS, NEXT AISLE"
   b. Take advantage of the fresh delight of children's art by turning their crayon, watercolor or felt-tip pen creations into a sign by over-marking with peel-off plastic letters, pin-back letters, adhesive letters, etc.
   c. Discover (or re-discover) the simple joys of rubber stamp letter sets found in most stationery or hobby shops and stamp pad yourself into business with any message you want to impart in a zany fashion.
   d. Depending on the need, dazzle (outline letters with glue, then sprinkle with glitter); go homespun (outline letters with glue, then trace with yarn or string); be rustic (outline letters with glue, then place toothpicks or slivers of wood in squared-off fashion on brownish poster board); grab-bag it (cut out letters from various bits of cloth, glue on fabric, stretch into a frame).
   e. Use unique backgrounds for traditional lettering (cloth, rugs, textured paper, photographs, splatter paint pictures, prints of masterpieces, etc.)
   f. Be as imaginative as you want,--woodburning, embroidery (remember those "Home Sweet Home" samplers?), needlepoint, banners of felt, follow the numbered dots--for make-it-yourself signs, etc.
   g. Borrow stand-up displays from retail businesses and turn them into something special for your library.
   h. Use photographs of patrons to "show" your message.

6. Multiple copies of a sign
   a. You have to adhere to copyright rules if you plan to make more than one copy of a sign.
   b. There are several kinds of office-type sign-making devices that permit you to make several copies after you have set the type or created a stencil or master (check office supply catalogs and local stores for equipment.)

7. Signs in braille
   a. This is an expected fact. Inexpensive braillers of appropriate size are available commercially or can be procured through the Talking Book Service available to all libraries.
   b. You may need to educate seeing patrons to the importance of leaving braille signs intact, especially in elevators for floor designations and instructions, and for floor plans.

STEP 36: UNIQUE WAYS OF DISPLAYING SIGNS.

Effective readership of a sign involves contents, design and placement. If placed too high, on an open door, in back of a planter or on the shadow side of a shelf, the medium and the message are lost. Signs can be a silent librarian, but they must be seen.

1. <u>Commercially produced sign holders</u> are available from any number of catalogs or art supply shops. Take the time to look, compare and experiment. Keep a list of such outlets:

COMMERCIAL OUTLETS FOR SIGN DISPLAY EQUIPMENT

NAME	ADDRESS	ITEMS	COMMENTS

2. <u>Standard self-help</u> sign display techniques
   a. Attach sign with rolled masking tape at the four corners (and in-between)
   b. Create a back-stand, as on a picture frame
   c. Attach to a dowel rod, hang by string attached to dowel rod ends (as with towel calendars)
   d. Tape two boards across the top, open up as an inverted "V" or a tent, so messages can be seen from two directions

3. Start on the road to thinking about the unusual
   a. Put the message in the form of a mobile--hang singly or in groups
   b. Create sign posts, either out of natural architectural elements (support beams) or by making your own (discarded coat racks are quite useful)
   c. Place signs on the floor--string out vinyl lettering that can survive traffic, use mystic tape arrows, vinyl footsteps, sets of string ...
   d. Create 3-dimensional signs that are self-supporting, like a piece of sculpture
   e. Utilize the ends and backs of bookshelves
   f. Anchor tree limbs into large planters and hang messages from the limbs
   g. Use dressed mannequins, stuffed-rag figures, stuffed gloves, scarecrows, etc. to hold messages
   h. Utilize any kind or variety of architectural features of the building (alcoves for hidden messages: "HAVE YOU SEEN THE MYSTERY IN THE MYSTERY SECTION?" --create a fun kind of mystery, like all of the Sherlock Holmes books are missing!)
   i. Frame the message inside a lovely frame and hang it in the arts section
   j. Create a record jacket message to place in the recording section
   k. Slip a clear-cut message inside a clear glass bottle and have the bottle and message "discovered"
   l. Try a cloth sign inside an embroidery hoop
   m. Turn a discarded book into a sign by slipping the message between

the cover and a new plastic wrap

n. Utilize old game boards to pass the word (paste the message down) --scrabble letters, monopoly instructions, etc.
o. Use stuffed animals to hold message balloons
p. Hang a saucepan with a message affixed to the bottom or to the inside or to both places
q. Borrow an idea from the Scandinavian Library Center and use an insert in among the books on shelves (as someone browses, there's a message!)
r. String up a line, hang your sign with spring clothespins
s. Cover a hoola-hoop with fabric, paint on a message, hang it from the ceiling

STEP 37: WHERE DO YOU NEED SIGNS?

Take a walking tour of your library. Specifically look for gaps in information-giving that could be improved with a sign.

SIGN INVENTORY--WHAT'S NEEDED

MESSAGE	LOCATION	SIZE	COLOR	HOW TO ATTACH

PART VII: DISPLAYS, EXHIBITS AND BULLETIN BOARDS

INTRODUCTION

Basically, the whole library should be on display, and like a flower garden, it should bloom in an array that is pleasing to all of the people who pass through. By definition, there is the merest shade of difference between "display" and "exhibit." By practice, there is a distinct differentiation. A display is far more informal, an exhibit is a much more ambitious undertaking. In the same way, there are bulletin boards and there are bulletin boards. Some are cork-backed surfaces upon which items of interest are tacked. Some are artistic developments.

Some general guidelines for displays, exhibits and bulletin boards

1. Have a clearly stated reason for creating a display, exhibit or bulletin board.

2. Make each visually pleasing--not too much or too little.

3. Use commercial lettering and typewriter print--do not hand letter unless you are an expert. Use the same style lettering for captions and copy.

4. Be alert to glare in glass cases.

5. In open spaces put only those objects that won't be harmed if touched.

6. Use different approaches--effectiveness is lost if the same layout, design or style is used over and over.

7. Plan the program (schedule) of displays, exhibits and bulletin boards so you are only working on one at a time. Do not get into a situation where every display needs to be changed on the same day. Arrange the schedule so that you are dismantling, storing and putting up one at a time. This means not using every space for Halloween. Instead, plan a variety, which might include "The Autumn Sky," "Football," "Falling Leaves" in addition to the traditional goblins and pumpkins. Refer to a calendar of significant events, etc., to plan ahead. Make up a sheet that guides you and your staff:

SPACE	TOPIC	WHO IS RESPONSIBLE	DATE UP	DATE DOWN	STORAGE AREA

8. Create an idea file--the best winter ideas come in the heat of summer! Develop a filing system that allows for easy retrieval (by months, seasons, topic ...).

9. Create a caption file. One idea often leads to another. Borrow from the world of commercials. If "THINGS GO BETTER WITH BOOKS" sounds good, write it down and let the idea simmer a while until a coming together occurs--one day you wake up and you have this great bulletin board that exactly fits that caption.

10. Anything, no matter how clever, loses impact if it stays around too long.

11. Good composition is important. Experiment with shapes. Observe magazine layouts to get the feel of how spatial relationships are used to focus on the main idea. Watch what color does to change mood and reaction. Notice that simplicity in design is more attractive than a cluttered, no-focus, everything-including-the-kitchen-sink approach. Be attentive to proportion.

12. Incorporate humor. Sometimes the statement that exaggeration makes is remembered longer than is a totally factual comment. How about mobs of people crushing up against each other to get a library card? Borrow a pop poster of Uncle Sam saying "JOIN NOW" and create an army of people with borrowed book in hand.

13. Take a photo of all of your displays, exhibits and bulletin boards before they are dismantled and someone comments--"Gosh, that was really clever, we should have taken a photo."

14. If the display, exhibit or bulletin board can be used again, pack the parts together, label and include the sketch.

15. In dismantling a display, exhibit or bulletin board, salvage parts that can be re-used for another purpose.

16. Develop a "prop box" which can contain all kinds of items and objects that are useful for displays, exhibits and bulletin boards. This includes backing materials, boxes of various sizes and kinds to create levels, fabrics for covering or highlighting, stands, frames, racks, bricks....

17. Develop topics that are of current interest to people in your service area. Some will appeal to specific groups, some to a general audience. Think business, industry, government, school, etc. as well as the arts.

18. Keep a card file of the location, size (measure it), special attributes and special problems of spaces within the library that can be used for displays, exhibits or bulletin boards. In this way new employees are aware of what's what. This also helps "guest" artists.

STEP 38: DISPLAYS.

1. <u>Use of displays.</u>

    a. Displays are a three-dimensional means of advertising:
        new materials, services.
        seasonal materials, services.
        materials, services that go along with a "special month."
        materials, services that fit in with community activities.
        the library as a whole.
        a specific aspect or program of the library.

    b. By placing an item out of its usual spot on a shelf, circulation can be increased.

    c. By placing items in unusual combinations (nutrition and sports) new interests can be sparked.

2. <u>Kinds of displays.</u>

    a. Displays can be locked-in materials (no touching), including:
        permanent display cases built into the library.
        moveable curio-type cabinets.
        borrowed glass cases for a special display.

    b. Displays can be traveling from one area of the library to another or from library to library or to various locations outside of the library.

    c. Displays can be free-standing, hands-on, on tables, on shelf tops, in corners, on chairs, in windows, hung on strung-up clothes line, propped against an easel ... or wherever and whatever the imagination permits.

    d. Displays can be arranged by library staff members or brought in by members of the community.

3. <u>Policies regarding displays.</u> There should be a written set of policies regarding displays so that the staff has guidelines. Items to include are:

    a. Patrons may/may not borrow materials on display.

    b. Patrons may sign up for materials on display. Dates are specified.

    c. Purchase and maintenance of cases and materials and payment of staff time are part of the regular budget.

    d. Expenditures for traveling displays are part of the budget.

    e. Insurance for items is written into the regular policy or as a rider to the regular policy.

4. Organizing a display schedule for local groups in the library.

   a. It may sound like an easy way out to have various local groups fill up the glass cases and shelf-tops in the library, but without organization this PR activity can backfire. If "Group A" doesn't remove its materials when "Group B" is ready to put its display up, hard feelings may result. Create an organizational chart:

NAME OF ORGANIZATION	PERSON IN CHARGE	TEL. #	THEME OF EXHIBIT	LOCATION	DATE UP	DATE DOWN

   b. Discuss the theme and content of each display before it is booked into the library. If it is of such a nature that is not in keeping with the general acquisition policies of the library, it might be wise to suggest an alternate display or simply politely thank the group for asking. It could also be that the theme is precisely the same as one that has already been booked in so that you will want to evaluate whether this situation would be an in-depth coverage or a redundancy. Determine any special needs to set up the display. Determine the time needed to set up and dismantle.

   c. Have a system of reminders set-up so that you can check on an organization that may have signed up six months ago, and with only a month away, you want to be sure they still remember.

   d. Arrange for adequate news media coverage of displays.

   e. Send a note of appreciation after the display is down.

   f. Co-ordinate a display with the library's materials and services.

   g. At times evaluate the impact displays have on library use.

5. Planning and setting up displays in the library by library staff.

   a. Displays in a case:
      1) Check on lighting, replace burned out bulbs.
      2) Clean the glass and dust the interior.
      3) Check for safety--will the case support the weight of the items, will care need to be taken to keep people from leaning on or bumping into the case.
      4) Check locks, if they are needed to protect the items on display.
      5) Assemble all the items that fit the theme and purpose you have articulated.

6) Sketch where in the space available each item should go. Omit some items if it starts to look like too much.
7) Arrange items according to the sketch.
8) Provide the necessary titles, copy, explanation, credits, etc., using your best techniques in sign-making.
9) Step back and look at the display as a patron would. Work at it to make it right.
10) Clean fingerprints away daily. Set anything aright that has fallen down.

b. Displays on tables:

1) Define the area of the table with fabric or fixtures that help draw attention to the display.
2) Use materials that patrons may handle. If it's out, it will be touched.
3) Provide for alternate materials to add to the display as items are borrowed.
4) Follow items 5-9 above.
5) Provide for interest through levels (achieved by using boxes that are covered or blocks of wood that are nicely varnished).
6) Borrow ideas for arrangements from retail stores--displays sell for them.

c. Displays on shelf tops and on shelves, between books:

1) Dust the shelf.
2) Provide for safety so that materials don't come tumbling down.
3) Make this an informal, spontaneous type of display, that adds pleasure to browsers. Perhaps you can pull materials from another section to act as teasers, with a note--"If you dig fiction, you won't want to miss the stranger-than-fiction stories in the biography section --just turn right at the end of these shelves" .... or whatever.
4) Place pieces of art, a mass of driftwood, an intriguing sea shell, a fish bowl, a suggestion box, an arrangement of new bookmarks ... on shelves.
5) Switch these tiny oases around to lend variety.

d. Displays on ledges or the tops of tall shelving:

1) Because these places are in a poor range of vision and out of reach of most patrons, use these spots for a decorative purpose rather than making circulating materials more appealing.
2) Some plants do well trailing off high places, or use seasonal materials.

e. Window displays:
   1) Use only those materials that won't be affected by sun (non-fade, fadeless).
   2) Use materials in proportion to the window size.
   3) Decide on open back, where one can see through to the interior, or closed back, where the backing is part of the display.
   4) Create a large shadow box effect with custom-made wooden shelving. Don't add a back, thus allowing a "see through" effect. See illustration no. 25.

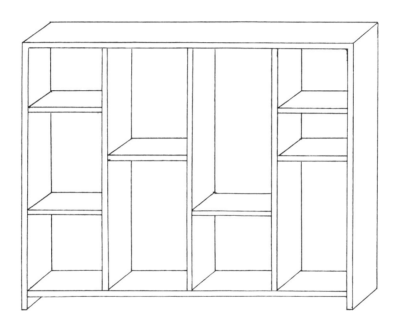

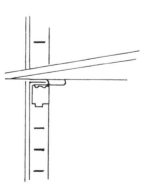

25. Book-size Shadow Box for
     Window Display

5) Check the display daily from the outside to make sure items haven't fallen, pages flipped or signs or lettering dropped off.
6) Aim for the dramatic, the extra-ordinary for the front window --this brings people in, just as it does for retail operations.

   f. Displays that hang:
1) Mobiles are attractive and can be created from any numbers of items.
2) Be unusual--create a papier-mâché figure, string it up securely, and let your ideas fly--figuratively.
3) Use household objects to attract attention. (If you have a dozen new cookbooks, hang a strainer, with this legend attached "Why strain your brain, Look in a Book to combine nutrition and meal planning with fun in eating....")

   g. Displays that stop you short:
1) Put up a scarecrow and surround it with gardening books.
2) Create a fortune teller out of stuffed clothing, set her in front of a crystal ball and have her say (via a sign): "I predict a tall, dark book in your future."
3) Bring in a motorcycle, park it and run a quiz on safety, the answers to which can be found in recent periodicals and news-papers.

   h. Traveling displays:
1) Aim primarily at a design that comes apart and puts together easily and travels well at the least cost.
2) Label everything, include a detailed sketch and repair kit to provide for the unexpected breakage. A photograph of the as-sembled display helps.
3) Attach precise instructions as to what comes apart and what doesn't.
4) Include all tools and label them for ownership.
5) Include an itemized check sheet to be filled in at the beginning and ending of the display schedule at each location.
6) Use clean packing materials. Avoid newspaper, which tends to rub ink on surfaces. Tissue paper, styrofoam, saved packing materials sent to the library, soft cloths, all work well.
7) Have a precise schedule of who has the display on which date and how and when it is to be transported. Note how long it will take to put up and dismantle.
8) Provide for news media coverage.

6. <u>Developing a "space program"</u> in your library.

Building on data from PART IV, and incorporating the material in this section determine key areas of patron traffic and designate them as target points to put up displays, exhibits or bulletin boards. But in-sist upon flexibility. Not all display areas should be permanent--more interest is created by a change of location. And, use your "outer space" to advantage, too. Everything need not be indoors if you have the kind of location that permits creative use of lawn for sculpture, landscaping for experiments in gardening, trees from which to hang lanterns (safely), etc. Take a look around, floorplan in hand, and be creative and adventurous.

STEP 39: EXHIBITS

1. Some general rules to follow

    a. A general exhibit should appeal to a variety of people and ages and should have a specific focus.
    b. The artistic development of an exhibit is as important as the contents. The exhibit must attract attention to itself and make a good immediate impression. Dimension, texture and motion attract attention.
    c. The background should enhance the materials on display, not be the main focus or a distraction.
    d. Borrowed items must be insured against breakage, theft, fire while on display and in transit.
    e. Usually, exhibits should be changed within $2\frac{1}{2}$-3 weeks (the average borrowing time for library materials), unless they are very special and large numbers of people need to have an opportunity to see them.
    f. Exhibit themes should be selected with consideration of the audience, date and location.
    g. Consider the effect of light, heat and other elements on items on display.
    h. Be aware of how long it takes to plan, set up, dismantle and store an exhibit. Allow for enough time.
    i. Keep captions and credits short and make them readable.
    j. Avoid clutter. Use open space to accentuate.
    k. If the exhibit warrants it, arrange for the printing of a catalogue, which can be sold or be available free of charge as a take home.
    l. If it is helpful, design a one-page guide to the exhibit.
    m. If the use of sound is not distracting, create a tape-recorded message to give background data and enhance the viewing. However, strive for a professional tape recording and script.
    n. Use sound effects and visual effects (slides, film-strips, film clips) if they enhance the exhibit.

2. Use of exhibits

    a. To tell the library's story for the purpose of creating understanding and goodwill prior to a bond issue or to commemorate a significant event or to celebrate an anniversary.
    b. To introduce services or materials.
    c. To demonstrate how to use the library's materials and services.
    d. To display special collections and ephemeral materials relating to them.
    e. To tie-in with things the people in the community are doing.

     f.   To enhance the image of the library as a community center.

     g.   As a service of the library, for other groups or individuals to bring in exhibits, the space being available free-of-charge.

3.   Kinds of exhibits

     a.   Portable shows
         1)   The complete exhibit can be taken apart, packed for transport and easily reassembled in any number of locations.
         2)   Follow steps as for a traveling display.
     b.   In-house
         1)   Use space that is accessible, that permits browsing (unlike a display, which usually warrants a quick look, exhibits require extra time to really examine all of it) and that accommodates a number of people at any one time.
         2)   Some ways to set up exhibits are in exhibit cases, on free standing panels, in windows, on easels, on table tops, on shelving, on walls, suspended from ceiling or beams.
     c.   Shows in malls, exhibition centers, fairs, department stores, airports, train and bus stations, and "wherever people assemble or pass by"
         1)   Capture attention and elicit action.
         2)   Make it sturdy to withstand public places.
     d.   Mobile shows
         1)   This includes vans, floats, bookmobiles, trucks, that go to where there are crowds of people.
         2)   Make only one statement that can easily be grasped and that will compete with the crush of the situation.

4.   Planning and setting up an exhibit

     a.   Decide on the main idea, purpose and target of the exhibit.
     b.   List the different items, materials and symbols that can be used to promote the central theme and purpose of the exhibit and note where they can be procured and what cost is involved.

THEME	CONTENTS	WHERE TO PROCURE	CONDITIONS	COST

Some basics to consider are:
1)   The items in the exhibit must be those that can be shown to their best advantage.
2)   The lettering must be compatible with the theme and scale of the exhibit.
3)   Motion can be created with an electric fan, a lazy susan, a turntable.
4)   Color should be compatible with the season and the mood as well as with the intent of the exhibit.

      5) Props can include the ordinary (pans and pots, tools) or the unusual (telephone booths, things out-of-context such as fashion store mannequins in a library setting).

      6) Memorabilia that adds interest can be anything from menus, sheet music, picture post cards, letters and greeting cards to original manuscripts.

      7) Background materials that enhance the exhibit may be woven mats, carpeting and peg board in addition to cloth or various kinds of paper.

  c. Determine the budget

  d. Work within the framework of the location and the audience to make decisions regarding the content of the exhibit. You need to know:

      1) What is the size of the area?

      2) What is the distance from which the exhibit will be seen?

      3) What type of audience will be viewing the exhibit--if the target is children, keep materials at a height comfortable for them.

      4) Will tables or cases be provided?

      5) What are the measurements of display areas for use?

      6) What type of lighting is available?

      7) Are there electric outlets? What is the capacity?

      8) Are spotlights available, and from what angles and heights?

5. Based on the location and space available, select those items (from the list above) that can best communicate the theme to the targeted audience.

6. Draw sketches of the exhibit, including the caption, lettering, props and central materials that you have decided upon. Some tips for good design include:

  a. Horizontal lettering is easier to read than is vertical.

  b. Simplicity in design is easier to follow than is complexity.

  c. Open space is essential.

  d. Elements that unite an exhibit:

    1) Repetition of color

    2) Repetition of shape

    3) Flow of line

    4) Style of lettering

    5) Compatibility of items to each other

  e. Elements that add drama (excitement) to an exhibit:

    1) Motion

    2) Layering of levels

    3) Bold colors

7. Construct fixtures or acquire the necessary tables, cases, etc.

8. Gather and prepare all materials necessary to construct the exhibit, based upon the sketch completed as a preparatory step in planning:

a. Prepare the background.
b. Mount all pictures, pamphlets, etc. with rubber cement on compatible boards cut to the right size, laminate or cover with clear acetate; attach tacks to the back with masking tape if these items are to be tacked up.
c. Specially prepare books that are to be mounted--remove a soiled or tattered jacket or protective plastic. Use a band of clear plastic to brace an open page.
d. Select lettering.
e. Prepare any secondary copy, including guides, catalogues and descriptions.
f. Enlarge items with the square method or with an enlarging, opaque, projector.

9. Assemble the exhibit.

a. Check all lights in cases or spotlights. Replace if necessary so all bulbs work.
b. Letter on a straight line by stretching string between two tacks as a guideline.
c. Securely anchor all items.

10. Check on the finishing touches:

a. Paint pin heads.
b. Clean away finger prints or smudges.
c. Proofread for errors in spelling or typing.
d. Straighten things that are crooked.
e. Snip loose strings.
f. Look for exposed stands, wires and cords that are safety hazards.
g. Conceal all hardware.

11. Photograph the exhibit and people involved with it.

12. Gather supplemental materials such as guides, directions, catalogues or tape-recorded messages and place where they belong in the exhibit.

13. Plan a publicity campaign which includes posters, flyers, etc. as well as news media.

14. Work on improving exhibit techniques by:

a. Making notes on exhibits that you see and that attract your attention.
b. Adding materials and props to the store room.
c. Jotting down ideas for future exhibits.
d. Shopping in lighting stores for different kinds of spotlights.
e. Being aware of ready-made exhibits and traveling exhibits.
f. Visiting museums to learn from them just as you learned display techniques from retail outlets.

15. Adapt the schedule in the display section to book in exhibits to the library.

STEP 40: BULLETIN BOARDS

1. Kinds of Bulletin Boards. Catalogs illustrate a variety, and imagination can fill in for a lot.

    a. Standard adhere to the wall cork variety.
    b. Moveable, two-sided.
    c. Sandwich boards made from plywood and cork overlay.
    d. Supporting posts turned into bulletin board space.
    e. Ends of shelving.
    f. Free-standing or table top figures, self-made or manufactured.
    g. Areas of carpeting on walls.
    h. Fabric on a dowel rod, hung as a banner (banner bulletin board).

2. Uses for Bulletin Boards

    a. Community Information
        1) Groups and individuals can post notices in accordance with the policy set by the Library Board.
        2) Library staff members take daily inventory to remove outdated material.
        3) If kept neat and up-to-date, it serves as an information exchange source.
    b. Library Information
        1) Public information about the library--minutes of board meetings, newspaper clippings, posters and notices of upcoming events, etc.--is available in a neat, attractive format.
        2) A daily inventory is needed to weed outdated material.
    c. Artistic development of a theme on a flat surface
        1) Find ideas for these kinds of bulletin boards by looking in a variety of periodicals (magazines), professional journals, coloring books, advertisements, greeting cards, picture books, bulletin board books, posters, or anything that catches your eye. Always be on the lookout for ideas. When you find one, cut it out or write it down and save it.
        2) File ideas under a system for easy retrieval--holidays, seasons, special weeks or months, topics, themes, or whatever. Don't wait until you need an idea to go hunting.
        3) Decide upon the purpose and theme for the bulletin board.
        4) Decide on the central point of interest. Every good bulletin board needs an eyecatcher.
        5) Decide on a caption that is easy to read or do without one if the message is clear otherwise.
        6) Sketch your idea according to the size and shape of the space available. If you do the sketch on a 3x5 or 5x7 card you file it for future use. List the materials needed and any other basic information.

7) Gather materials. Save a lot of time by creating a storage space for bulletin board materials that are basic --background, fadeless paper, fabrics, textured paper, borders, yarn, findings from nature, etc.

8) Set up the bulletin board. A good start is a background cover of solid color fadeless paper or fabric. Next, add the central point of interest, the caption and any other copy. Finally, add finishing touches.

3. Tips for Bulletin Boards

a. Real objects always attract attention.
b. Positive and negative can provide a unifying background for displaying many small notices, photographs, or an audience (patron) response section (such as letting people know what happened to suggestions that were placed in the suggestion box).
c. Keep them current.
d. Allow for patron participation (color in, create an object based on a theme, write a caption....)
e. For visual weight, most items should be in the lower half.

PART VIII: INK PRINT ADVERTISING

STEP 41: GENERAL OVERVIEW

There are several options for reproducing material. The best way to determine which process to use for each job that you have is for you to make an appointment to visit with several kinds of printers and to learn from each their capabilities, their requirements for copy preparation and their scale of costs. A check of the telephone directory yellow pages under "Printers" will reveal these processes: LETTERPRESS, OFFSET (LITHOGRAPHY), SILK SCREENS, ENGRAVING (INTAGLIO), SPEED PRINTING. Some will specialize in what they print, such as business forms, business cards, invitations, announcements, posters, letter heads, newsletters, brochures, commercial printing.

1. Processes for duplication:

   a. Letterpress is most often associated with printing newspapers and magazines. Copy (the written matter) has traditionally been set by typographers and linotype operators. The high cost of these crafts-people, however, has led to an increased use of phototypesetting and computerized typesetting. In letterpress you give the printer copy and art work to fit a specific layout that you design. You choose the typeface, the quality and color of paper and the color of ink. A job may be one color or many colors of ink.

   b. Offset lithography, because its cost is lower than letter press, is now more often used for printing newspapers and is a preferred printing process for newsletters, brochures and bookmarks. Offset has a capability for printing in a variety of ink colors and paper stocks. Offset printers will work from "camera ready" originals which you prepare or they will have their typography department set the type and have their graphic artist provide the layout according to your specifications.

   c. If you want engraved stationery or invitations you use Intaglio printing.

   d. Silk screen, once extremely expensive, is now more attractive cost-wise. It is a good process for posters and book covers. The design must be given to the printer. You choose the colors of ink and paper.

e. Speed printing works from "camera ready" copy to reproduce in black ink on a choice of paper colors and paper stock.

f. Office photo-copying can be similar to speed-printing in the finished product, which is always black ink on a variety of paper colors.

g. Stencil duplicating can be simple black and white or provide for a variety of ink changes. Check office supply stores for what is available.

h. Spirit duplicating machines usually means blue "ink" on white paper, but a capability of masters with a variety of colors can offer alternatives. Again, check office supply stores for what is available.

i. A growing variety of in-house duplicating possibilities can be investigated on a shared facility or shared use basis.

2. Type styles
   (See illustration no. 26 on following page):

a. Serif: those styles that have a fine cross-stroke at the top or bottom of each letter.

b. Sans-serif: those styles with no cross-stroke.

c. Within these are three classes: black letter (sometimes called gothic), roman and italic. See illustration no. 27 on following page.

d. Decorative, Modern and Display are styles that fall into categories not pegged by serif or sans-serif. There are hundreds of typefaces, each with its own name. Depending upon the method that you use, you can make choices from a variety of catalogs.

e. Typewriter typefaces come in a variety, too, depending upon the choice of machine and its capabilities for interchangeable elements. Choose a style that is right for the duplicating process that you plan to use. Read the catalog thoroughly before making final selections.

3. Type sizes

    a. Height is measured in points (the smallest unit). Twelve points equal one pica in the English-American system of measuring; 1 pica = .1660" (4.217mm). The range can be from 3 point on up: 8 point is what you see in some dictionaries; 12 point is comfortable reading size; 36 point is often for headlines; and 96 point may appear in display advertising. See illustration no. 28.

    b. Width is described as standard (normal), condensed, extra-condensed and extended. It is measured by how many letters fit into an inch of space. See illustration no. 29.

    c. Typewriter type is referred to as pica or elite and usually has the capability of producing 10 or 12 letters per inch. See illustration no. 30.

4. Type descriptions. See illustration no. 31 for examples of Capitals, Small Capitals and lower-case letters. (If this quick overview has peaked your interest, you can satisfy all kinds of curiosity in any number of books on the subject of type and typefaces.)

5. Copy form. Copy is any reading matter.

    a. Flush left, justified type-- most common for printer-set type, as in books, newspapers, magazines:

        XXXXXXXXXXX
        XXXXXXXXXXX
        XXXXXXXXXXX
        XXXXXXXXXXX
        XXXXXXXXXXX

26. Serif   Sans-serif

27. Gothic   Roman Italic

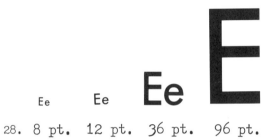

28. 8 pt. 12 pt. 36 pt. 96 pt.

29. Extra   Condensed Standard Extended
    Condensed

PICA   ELITE
pica   elite

30. Pica   Elite

ABCDE   ABCDE   abcde

31. Capitals Small Capitals lower case

b. Flush left, ragged right edge--most common for typewritten material, as in letters:

```
XXXXXXXXXXXX
XXXXXXXXXXX
XXXXXXXXXXXXXX
XXXXXXXXXXX
XXXXXXXXXXXX
```

c. Flush right, ragged left edge--used in brochures, flyers, posters:

```
XXXXXXXXXXXX
    XXXXXXXXX
XXXXXXXXXXXXX
    XXXXXXXXXX
```

d. Stepped lines--each line is the same width but each is moved to the right a specific number of spaces:

```
XXXXXXXXXXX
   XXXXXXXXXXX
     XXXXXXXXXXX
       XXXXXXXXXXX
```

e. Vertical lines--copy that must be read down instead of across. It is best used one line at a time for accent rather than as body type to avoid confusion of the message:

```
B  A  F
O  R  R
O  E  I
K     E
S     N
      D
      S
```

f. Novelty--type set into a recognizable shape, such as a tree, a house, a silhouette of a famous person, a flag, etc. (There are books of patterns for these.) You merely fit the message into the shape.

6. Kinds of art work

a. Photographs. Black and white glossy prints duplicate best unless you are printing in color.

b. Hand art. There is a wide span including pen and ink, halftones, charcoal, acrylics, oil, water colors, wash, etc. and including engravings. (If you use work by young patrons, with a credit line, you will get attention simply because people care about this. Sometimes you do need professional work so keep a file of local people, their specialities and their charges.)

c. Clip art. Buy from professional art work services with free reproduction rights. Check ads in professional library journals.

7. Reasons for using art work

a. As a visual explanation (show how to use a tape player).

b. As an attention getter (arrow in center of bull's eye--caption reads: "BE ON TARGET--USE YOUR LIBRARY").

c. As a message itself (photo of elderly person contentedly listening to a talking book in a library setting).

8. Paper

a. <u>Bond Papers</u>
   1) consist of weights that range from 16 pounds (16#) to 24# with 20# being the most common and usually used for letterheads (office stationery).
   2) typed by content. Sulfate (wood pulp): No. 1 for watermarked paper; No. 2, No. 3, No. 4 for economical typewriter paper. Made in stronger colors in addition to white and pastels. Rag content (graded by percentage of rags--can go up to cloth paper): 25% rag is most common; made in white and pastels.
   3) available in various textures

b. <u>Offset Papers</u> (Book Papers)
   1) Range from 50# to 80#:
      50# offset is the same as 20# bond (for weight);
      60# offset is the same as 24# bond;
      60# and 70# are the most commonly used offset papers.
   2) available in different finishes:
      vellum finish has a "tooth" to it;
      smooth finish;
      gloss finish (also called enamel); 70# gloss offset is most often used for magazines.
   3) comes in a wide range of colors and textures.

c. <u>Cover Stock Papers</u>
   1) Used mainly for covers

2) Most paper manufacturers make an offset sheet with a matching cover stock
3) Weight range is from 55# to 80#; 65# is the most popular
4) Available in smooth or vellum in varieties of colors and textures to match and contrast with offset papers

d. <u>Index Papers</u> (Bristol Papers or Bristol Board) (Card Stock)
1) Available in 90# to 140#; 110# is the most common (3x5 card weight)
2) Thickness is measured by ply: 90# = 2 ply; 110# = 3 ply; 140# = 4 ply
3) Heavier weights are used for posters
4) 110# (3 ply) is the maximum weight that small offset presses can handle
5) Silkscreen print shops can handle any weight (you will most often go to them for the very heavy weight posters)
6) Letterpress print shops can most economically print weights between what offset and silkscreen can
7) Comes in pastel colors only
8) Index and Card Stock have a smooth, slick surface
9) Bristol is textured (more economical than index; has less body) 67# Bristol is the minimum Postal Service weight as a self-mailer

e. <u>Office papers</u>

1) Mimeograph bond
2) Spirit duplicator paper
3) Gestetner paper
4) Copier paper

9. Color

a. Use color to attract, identify and create aesthetic appeal.

b. In an on-going campaign, it is good to establish a specific color of paper and ink with that particular service, product, program or message. In this way, even if you send a flyer bulk rate, the addressee won't dump it out as "junk" mail, but will recognize it as the monthly VIP mailer from the library; or if it's a handout around town, the interested audience will naturally pick it up to learn what that month's calendar of events includes, etc.

c. Certain colors of paper are better than others for duplicating art work in speed printing processes. Ask to see samples before you make decisions.

d. Combinations of colors create different effects and moods. Know your objective and make choices accordingly. The visual image you project will precede and outlast the copy content. It may well determine whether or not the piece will be read at all.

10. Methods of distribution

    a. In the library
      1) At the circulation desk as a pick up
      2) In prepared packets for one-on-one distribution (New patron, tour group, class, program participants, VIPs, etc)
      3) Around the library in specific departments; on shelves, tables, bulletin boards or racks; in odd places--between books, in a planter, on a papier-mâché hand reaching out of the mystery section, in a bird cage in the pets section, under the lid of the copying machine, in the middle of a magazine.

    b. Outside of the library
      1) Pay envelopes at work
      2) Check out counters in retail stores
      3) Bank and utility mailings
      4) Take-homes for school children
      5) Handouts at recreational centers
      6) Foldovers at eating establishments
      7) Supplements to newspapers (local, school, organizations, churches, etc.)
      8) Door-to-door campaign give-away
      9) Malls, fairs, parades as pickups and handouts
      10) Direct mailings from the library to select audiences
      11) In bulk distributions to high traffic sites (bus stations)
      12) In information racks set up in specific locations
      13) In special deliveries to places of high population concentration (apartment complexes)

11. Reasons for creating ink print materials

    a. To announce

    b. To remind

    c. To introduce

    d. To entice

    e. To inform

    f. To seek support

    g. To maintain growth

    h. To solicit data

    i. To generate action

    j. To end rumors

    k. To start a tradition

l. To maintain a tradition

m. To attract attention

n. To beat out competition

o. To tie-in with an existing event

p. To commemorate

q. To celebrate

r. To make a statement

12. Basic rules across the board

a. Never do anything without planning (see "The Print Plan Outline," p. 87).

b. Have full data on hand before you start designing ink print materials.

c. Define your purpose for each piece--what is that piece supposed to do?

d. Build in an evaluation in the purpose, design and distribution.

e. Target a specific audience or segment of population and design the piece to reach that group.

f. Once again, work for ACCURACY, BREVITY, CLARITY: use one word instead of two; use simple sentences, catchy phrases, attention-getting headlines; use words everyone will understand and that have a universal meaning; double-check data, spelling and use of language.

g. Simple, clear, direct advertising is your best sales agent. Leave off superlatives, gushiness, claims you can't substantiate. Use white space effectively.

h. Image-building takes place through your ink print materials. Take a good look at what you just put together--is that the image you want to project?

i. Market-test everything before it goes into production. Assemble a group of people from various segments and groups--be sure each will be honest and not just say everything is "fine." Show them every design in its sketch stages--get reactions. Re-design accordingly (don't get defensive--don't argue--listen and learn).

j. What is special about your library? Establish your image around that.

k. Advertise what you can successfully deliver. Accentuate your positive aspects.

l. Apply all the essentials of good business advertising to your library. Get out--look around--see what's working for others and cleverly adapt; look at what comes in your mail--evaluate it, re-design, test, use.

m. Make everything you do count--the rule in business is that only half of what is spent brings in a return, but which half? Libraries can learn to target ink print materials to score better.

n. Is it worthwhile considering multi-lingual materials for some of your audience?

o. Use cooperative library publicity:
   1) share with neighboring libraries
   2) assign a clerk or a library volunteer the task of going through each professional journal the moment it comes in to send for "free" and "inexpensive" materials, including publishers' promotional bookmarks, posters, samples, materials exchanges, etc.
   3) ask for and use promotional materials made available by jobbers who supply you with materials for circulation
   4) order out of catalogs

p. Anticipate the needs of patrons--create or provide materials that the people who use the library need:
   1) scratch pads for note-taking (convenient 3x5 size with library logo)
   2) small pencils with the library imprint (borrow an idea from the golf course)
   3) imprinted plastic bags for rainy day carry homes
   4) pre-printed shopping lists with library imprint
   5) pre-printed excuses, with library imprint:
       _____ was absent from school on _____ because _____
       signed _____
       date _____
   (design a whole batch for all sorts of reasons.)

q. Put the library's name, address, tel. no., and hours on everything you print.

r. Inject humor and lightness wherever it is appropriate.

s. As in mass media material, link as much as you can locally-- people are naturally more interested in themselves and their neighbors than in people 500 or 1000 miles away. Tell local library success stories, use the art work and poster designs of local talent through contests, get local testimonials and get local coverage in state or national outlets.

t. Work with advertising and PR professionals when and if it is to the library's advantage, but the library publicity coordinator should always be in command. Ask to see examples of their work, establish all costs and read and verify any contract before signing anything.

u. Be realistic and positive. Tell people what the benefits are to them in specific rather than idealistic terms--use statistics to show that people who read and engage in self-study advance more rapidly in their jobs than do people who make no effort to grow or that parents who read influence their children to do so, and these are the young people who more readily succeed in a classroom situation.

v. Personalize in the words you choose--even in a bulk mailing or a large run of bookmarks use YOU are invited, YOUR library, one of a series to fit YOUR needs

w. Be creative within the bounds of what your target audience considers tasteful and appealing.

x. Never send out anything you would not be pleased and proud to receive yourself. Always feel good about your work.

y. Establish 100 percent staff support for any item that carries the library's name. Lack of enthusiasm can kill a program before it ever gets started.

13. Basic components of the ink print budget

a. Staff time to generate the idea

b. Staff time to carry out the operations from idea to action

c. Actual cost of the design and printing operations

d. Actual cost of distribution

e. Actual cost of evaluation

f. Cost of purchasing ready-made materials

14. Forms of ink printed materials

a. Flat (as in a sheet or leaf)

b. Folded (see illustration no. 32) (cont'd. on p. 89)

THE PRINT PLAN OUTLINE   date___/___/___
                                          dept._____

TOPIC_____

BASIC DATA_____

         _____

REASON (OBJECTIVE)_____

BUDGET_____

TARGET AUDIENCE_____

DISTRIBUTION OPTIONS_____

SIZE_____   COLOR_____

MEDIUM_____

MESSAGE_____

DESIGN IDEAS

MARKET TEST PROCDURE_____
PRINTING PROCESS_____

TIME LINE | WHO IS IN CHARGE OF EACH STEP?

  distribution date_____|_____

  pick up from printer_____|_____

  deliver to printer_____|_____

  complete design & pasteup___|_____

  gather data_____|_____

  initiate planning_____|_____

EVALUATION MECHANISM_____

_____

RESULTS OF EVALUATION_____

_____

LINK-UP TO LONG RANGE PLAN_____

_____

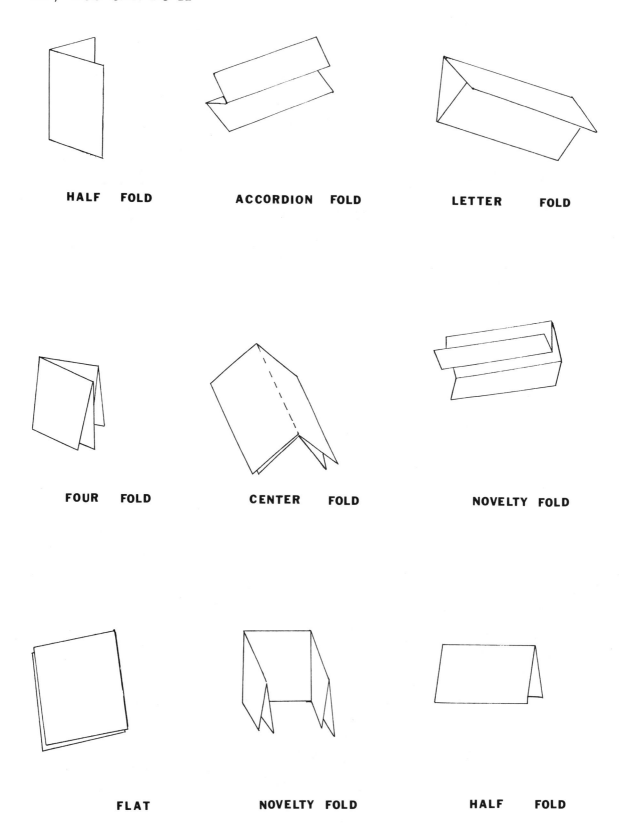

HALF FOLD   ACCORDION FOLD   LETTER FOLD

FOUR FOLD   CENTER FOLD   NOVELTY FOLD

FLAT   NOVELTY FOLD   HALF FOLD

32. Kinds of Folds for Printed Materials

1) letter fold
2) accordion fold
3) center fold
4) half fold (single fold)
5) four fold (French fold)
6) novelty fold

c. Book (the number of pages and binding determine the exact terminology)

STEP 42: INK PRINT POSSIBILITIES

1. <u>Announcements</u>

   a. Formal, engraved or embossed cards to announce an important event like the opening of a time capsule sealed 100 years ago, the retirement of the library director with a 25-year tenure, or a building dedication, etc.

   b. Informal, photo offset to announce anything from a new service to a change in circulation procedure to a vacancy on the library board. The content possibilities depend entirely upon the person sending it:

   XTOWN LIBRARY IS HAPPY TO ANNOUNCE THE

   ARRIVAL OF COMPUTERIZED CIRCULATION

   YOU WILL BE PLEASED ABOUT THE FOLLOWING IMPROVEMENTS

   AS A RESULT---

   c. These can be flat sheets used as broadsides or folded for mailing or for pick-up.

2. <u>Annual Reports</u>

   a. Can be anything from books to bookmarks.

   b. Its basic purpose is to tell all taxpayers
      1) what the library has done
      2) what the library is doing
      3) what the library plans to do

   c. Content and style are determined by the objective and theme.
      What do you want to tell to whom in what way? Example:
         Objective: Show how the library has reached more groups of people this year
         Theme: The Library and Xtown are good for each other
         Contents--Letter from the Library Board President

--Financial information/operational data. As productivity (wider use) went up, cost per transaction went down
--Transaction statistics. Circulation, telephone reference, walk-in use, outreach, programming
--User profiles: testimonials
--Personnel: Board members, library staff, Friends, Volunteers, Boosters, Donors, Committees, Corporate authority
--Summary and Forecast

d. Graphs can be used effectively to show much of the above so as to cut down on the blocks of copy. Illustration no. 33 could represent trends of circulation and library use from 19 __ -19 __.

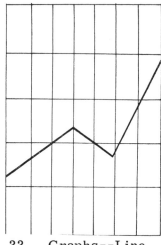

33.   Graphs--Line

e.   Charts can make difficult concepts easy for everyone to grasp. Illustration no. 34 could show how the library tax dollar is spent.

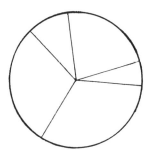

34.   Chart--Pie

e. (cont.) Illustration no. 35 could show growth of public participation in the library operation.

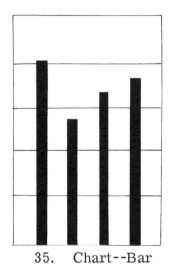

35. Chart--Bar

Illustration no. 36 could be used to represent library users in relation to the total population.

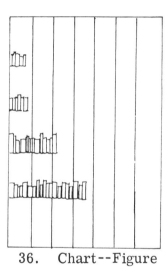

36. Chart--Figure

f. Maps can show locations of target areas within the community where the greatest use increases occurred and areas in the library that received the largest amount of traffic.

g. Photographs, taken all year long, can document what went on
   1) special recognition to employees for 5, 10, etc. years of service
   2) special recognition to volunteers for hours of service
   3) special recognition to patrons who signed up another library user
   4) special recognition to segments of the population that boosted the library
   5) staff in action
   6) programs and services that had high visibility
   7) media people on the job telling the library story
   8) autographing party for a local author

    h.   Produce a special annual report for young people in a format and style attractive to them.

        1) one continuing idea is to tell a facet of the library story each year (who chooses books and why; what makes a book a reference tool; etc.)

        2) print extra copies to satisfy future requests

    i.   Begin planning annual reports at least a year ahead so that all the materials are ready when it is countdown time to the printer.

    j.   Collect annual reports from all sorts of places to get ideas.

    k.   Use the front and back covers effectively to catch interest and tell a story visually.

3.   <u>Answer sets</u>

    a.   Anticipate the kinds of requests for information that users want (or begin to catalog the questions about library materials, services and operation that reoccur) and create printed materials that can be given or sent to provide answers. Examples: "I have a three-year-old niece, what kinds of books should I get her for her birthday?" "Where do I find your telephone books for other cities?" "How do I sign up for those craft classes you've been advertising?"

    b.   Prepare a nicely put together memo or tag-on that in essence says "thank you for asking--let us hear from you again...."

    c.   Daily update the answer sets to keep them current and timely--different seasons spur different kinds of questions and the answers to the same questions can change--including hours open and location of items.

    d.   Design materials that easily fit into an envelope and that can either be kept for ready reference or that can immediately, effectively answer the question.

4.   <u>Bags</u>

    a.   Carrying bags in various sizes, shapes and materials and with any number of messages have been recognized as effective modes of advertising the world over for many, many years.

    b.   Commercial sources with library imprints are available and can be checked out through catalogs that specialize in library supplies.

    c.   The cost can be underwritten as a public service project for a business or a local organization if the library wants to go that route.

    d.   Plastic or paper bags can be give-aways or sold for a minimal fee.

e. Cloth bags can be sold through the library gift shop or as a special project by Friends.

f. The more people seen carrying library bags, the more visibility for the library.

g. Adjuncts are library imprint scarves (squares of lighter fabric and winter weight) and umbrellas with the library imprint. They can be service give-aways for employees (along with bags) and volunteers and thus can become walking advertisements.

5. Books

a. It seems remote that the institution that deals with books will produce one, but it is not out of the question that as a PR tool a book is a possibility. It may be planned to mark an historical event or to provide a biography of a person who is a significant contributor to the community through the library, etc.

b. Depending upon the audience, the book should either be published locally with the library totally in charge or through a national publisher and distributed as a national publication.

6. Booklets, leaflets, pamphlets, handbooks

a. Number of pages and type of binding usually differentiate between the four kinds. The content determines how many pages, durability required of cover and paper, and design.

b. Pagination sometimes becomes a problem. The best way to determine what goes on which page is to fold blank pages into each other and to start numbering. (See illustration no. 37.)

c. Size depends upon need. Office duplicated materials can be $8\frac{1}{2}$"x 11" pages folded (each piece of paper, printed front and back, yields four pages) or legal size sheets folded. Commercially printed jobs can be scaled up and down in size.

d. The folding can be smack in half or arranged in a flip pattern. (See illustration no. 38.) Think of where the fold will be in arranging what goes on each page.

e. Learn by looking at what others have produced. Pick out what will work for your situation. Be attentive to readability, good use of art, overall design, readable type and the effect of color on the impression or mood you want to create.

7. Booklists

a. Put these on any mode of printed matter from booklets to bookmarks to folders to broadsides.

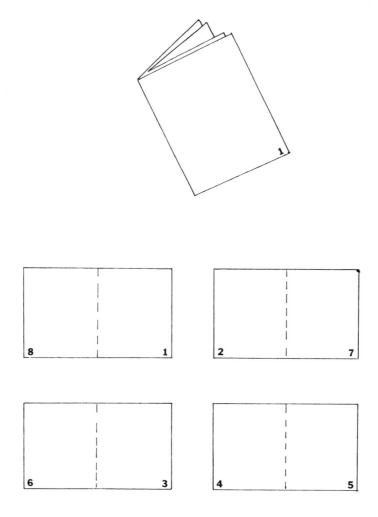

37.   Pagination in Planning Booklets, etc.

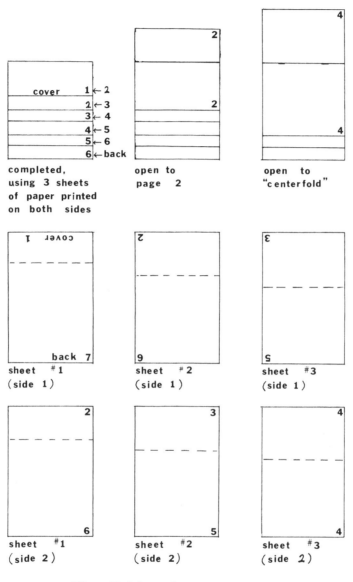

completed,
using 3 sheets
of paper printed
on both sides

open to
page 2

open to
"centerfold"

cover 1

back 7

sheet #1
(side 1)

2

9

sheet #2
(side 1)

3

5

sheet #3
(side 1)

2

6

sheet #1
(side 2)

3

5

sheet #2
(side 2)

4

4

sheet #3
(side 2)

38.   Folding for a Flip Chart
      or Pamphlet

b.   List the title clearly either in boldface type or underlined or in
     capital letters.

c.   List the author's name in natural order, first name then last name.

d.   If possible, an annotated listing is usually preferred, but make the
     description brief and capture the theme.   Avoid editorializing on the
     contents unless it is a review.

e. The possibilities are unlimited: Special subject listings; Recent books suggested by readers of Xtown Library; Works of an author in chronological order; Order of books in series (by author or topic); Media tie-ins.

f. Forecast and prepare in advance for reader demand (be on top of what is relevant and current to the patrons, be it localized or national).

g. Make the lists attractive, even if you expect them to be throw-aways. If you are typing them be certain to use a typewriter that has clean keys and a good ribbon.

8. <u>Bookmarks</u>

a. Cardstock is preferred, but there is much value in the mimeograph paper weight if the bookmark is to be used as an announcement of a program or a reminder of a service.

b. Commercially produced bookmarks available through library outlets are worth investigating and keeping in stock.

c. For your self-designed bookmarks let your creative juices bubble over:
   1) use size to make the initial impact--anything from long and skinny to four on an $8\frac{1}{2}$"x11" paper to three on the same size sheet
   2) choose lettering and color for the dramatic effect they can give
   3) put the message into non-conventional terms or use a cliché in a new way
   4) work art into the design--run a bookmark contest and reproduce the winning entries
   5) borrow and adapt ideas from other sources if they are not copyrighted

d. Make the product neat, legible and eye-catching:
   1) always sketch your design and plan out exactly how and where you want each part of the bookmark
   2) use commercial lettering, excellent handletters or a typewriter free from imperfections
   3) use commercially produced art (clip art), a photograph that has good reproduction qualities or original art that's special
   4) keep the paste-up clean (rubber cement pickup, soft eraser, blue pencil that does not reproduce on photo offset)

e. Use front and back if possible
   1) use the flipside as a teaser--ask a riddle, state a fact about the library, give a clue for a library scavenger hunt
   2) use the flip side to solicit patron response--ask a question about library materials or service (after a number of responses, publish the results: BOOKMARKS AS POLLSTERS ...)

f. Publish bookmarks in a series; number them.

g. Automatically include an informational bookmark in all materials checked out for circulation.

h. Some ideas (in addition to annual reports in brief and booklists): Recipes and menus (series); Notices of meetings and programs; Calendars of events; Nonsense and just plain fun.

9. Broadsides or flyers or handbills or circulars

a. These are single sheets of paper letter folded or accordian folded for handouts, pick-up distribution or self-mailers.

b. Can open up into small poster for bulletin board use.

c. Avoid sloppy, hurriedly scrawled pieces as you would the plague-- nothing belittles the library image faster than a tacky flyer--if the message is worth spreading, it's worth the little extra bit of time it takes to create an attractive piece with punch.

d. Basic production techniques:
    1) Make preliminary decisions regarding: what audience you want to reach; how you want them to respond; how much time and money you have for production; the method of distribution.
    2) Doublecheck the data: match up the day, date, year; specify am, pm, noon, midnight; spell all names correctly and use titles consistently; advertise only what you can really deliver; ask several people to proofread and market test for a clear message.
    3) Design with immediate appeal in mind.

10. Bulletins

a. Anything from a one-page flat sheet to a book.

b. It is the content that makes it a bulletin--while the broadside or flyer is usually an announcement, the bulletin is an official notice, a factual report or a collection of informative material.

c. Unlike the newsletter, it is issued irregularly and only when there is something special to communicate to a specific audience.

d. It is usually more austere and extremely business-like with the headline being the only art work.

e. It is usually reproduced on official letterhead or specially designed bulletin sheets.

f. The message must be clearly articulated.

11. <u>Buttons</u>

    a. Commercially produced with a special message, they are easy to purchase and distribute because people enjoy wearing them.

    b. Button makers are available at reasonable cost--simply follow the directions.

    c. Many communities have businesses that produce buttons. Check them out in the yellow pages and design your own to coordinate with a full advertising campaign that can include flyers, posters, banners, bulletin boards, etc.

12. <u>Calendars</u>

    a. Weekly or monthly listing of events on anything from bookmarks to inexpensively duplicated posters of any size.

    b. A month-by-month calendar with a whole year of library events specially marked in.

13. <u>Catalogs</u>

    a. Can be simple or elaborate, almost becoming a collector's item.

    b. The reason for the catalog dictates the form and number of pages.

    c. Some examples: with an exhibit; documenting a library's special collection.

    d. The cover is usually attractive and related to the contents.

    e. The overall design has to be coordinated with the subject.

14. <u>Coupons</u>

    a. A fast growing attraction item that cashes in on the economic signs of the times.

    b. Usually a good "Welcome Wagon" device: "Good for a Free Credit Card to Information--Present at Xtown Library, 123 Book Street any M-F 9am-9pm, Sat 9am-5pm, Sun noon-5pm." On the flip side, list the basic items in the collection.

    c. Can also be used with special programs--for a specific number of books read in a program a coupon is given. For a specified number of accumulated coupons, prizes (donated by businesses or groups) can be awarded.

15. <u>Comic books or comic strips</u>

a. A popular way of sharing information that might not be as attractive in any other way (unless you can afford computerized programming or a film strip that is custom designed for library use).

b. You can utilize local talent to create but the message must be clear and the characterizations have to be attractive to achieve holding power.

c. Library instruction is a good topic to tackle with the medium.

d. Black and white, with an invitation for the patron to color in, is a good, inexpensive duplicating process.

16. Computer letters

a. A way to individualize a mass message in a fraction of the time it takes to hand type each letter for a large group of people.

b. The contents of such a letter must be all things for all people if it is a blanket mailing. Some changes can be made to allow for group differences.

17. Fact (Informational) Sheets or Service Leaflets

a. The basic data resources of your library, constantly updated, designed to be saved and referred to by the patrons or as a handy item for visitors or as an information source for people in mass media.

b. Information is best presented in outline form, in an easy-to-read-and-retain design with clear type on paper that is middle grade-- too nice to throw away but not too expensive to freely distribute.

c. Basic data to include: name of library; address: street, city, state, zip; telephone numbers (specify departments); hours; circulation information; holdings; specifications on the building--floor plan; staff; community participation: Friends/Volunteers/Boosters; library board members/board meeting dates, place, time; programs and services; transportation facilities to the library.

d. In a series, separate pieces can emphasize specific areas within the library, bike paths, walking routes, spots to visit on a tankful of gas, local historical sites, etc., the child and the library (first visit, how to choose materials, "the sick child").

18. Gimmicks

a. With a little imagination, inexpensive items can go a long way to make the library a household word.

b. Some ideas for young patrons:

1) preprinted sheets the size of a pop (soda) can surface--patrons glue this sheet around the empty pop can to turn it into a coin bank. Slogan: "You Can Bank on Xtown Library for the Best in Reading, Listening and Looking." Design: simple but memorable. You can create all sorts of slogans on the savings angle.

2) preprinted sheets the size of a soup can surface--patrons glue this sheet around an empty soup can to make a pencil holder. Slogan: "Sharpen Your Skills at Xtown Library."

3) create a series of heavy cardstock rulers. Slogans: "Measure Up to Your Potential," "Inch Up to Success," "Use the Xtown Library Regularly," "Use the Xtown Library."

4) draw a page-full of Valentine's Day cards for young patrons to cut out and color (also, Father's Day, Mother's Day, Hallowe'en, etc). Slogan: "Who Knows What Good (Book) Lurks Inside the Library? (I'll Shadow You Until You're Mine)." Size the items to fit into standard envelopes for mailing.

5) flat print games and toys that people can take home and make:
TOPS: "Get In the Spin of Activities at Xtown Library" (print the calendar on the four-sides--include the library name, address, tel. no. and hours)
PLAY LIBRARY: Model of the Library; Dress Up Dolls for Patrons and Staff, etc.
CIRCULATION: Create a board game that goes through the steps of card catalog, Readers' Guide, stacks, and finally check out--base it on your floor plan (with diversions for: stopped off at program, looked at display case, examined a statue, got a drink of water, etc.)

6) interest the bank into running a series of local scenes on its checks--have one of them be the library (cooperate with other agencies in the area to pull this one off).

7) print those same scenes on placemat size paper--coat with plastic or have patrons do it on their own--great for coasters, too.

c. The trick for gimmicks is to create high visibility items at a low cost and to get them as widely spread around as possible--get people to come in to ask about them--get people involved in creating them--get a lot of media coverage--get enthusiastic and let it spread.

19. Guides; Flip Cards; Instruction Book

a. How-to's for use of any and everything in the library.

b. Extreme care must be taken not to use library jargon.

c. Can be printed as a flat sheet, as a middle fold or a tri-fold.

d. Must be eye-catching and give a positive image.

e. Flip cards can serve as a step-by-step procedure for running everything from a phonograph to a computer terminal or as a training device for using library materials e.g., (card catalog).

f. Can be stationery, affixed to a spot next to the item that needs explaining or comfortable enough to carry around from place to place throughout the library as a "silent" guide.

g. For the pre-literate or visually handicapped or blind patrons who need assistance, work up a program of guides on cassette tapes.

20. Handbooks; Employee manuals

a. Extremely important for library board, staff and volunteers.

b. Make it attractive, versatile (snap binder to permit slipping out of outdated data and replacement of updated information), easy to use and keep.

c. Include all pertinent topics from the by-laws to vacation specifications. Stress benefits and positive reinforcement.

d. Handbooks can also be adjuncts to programming, providing participants with a useful take-away or as a reference tool for people participating in a "DISPLAY IT AT THE LIBRARY" program so that they know the do's and don't's.

21. Inserts; stuffers

a. Specialized data on just the right size folded or single sheet to fit into pay envelopes, bank statements, store statements, etc.

b. Community groups, as a public service, will include library data in their regular mailings--but this is often a one-shot deal.

22. Invitations

a. Anything from the expected formalized engraved piece to a sheet of paper folded to $5\frac{1}{2}$"x$8\frac{1}{2}$" but which opens up to a gigantic wall poster with magnificent colors and breathtaking design.

b. Use what will get you the kind of response that you want--ask for "RSVP" if it is important to have a head count a specified number of days before the event.

c. The event will dictate the form of the invitation.

23. Labels

a. Address labels can have an impact--especially if they are eye-catching. Investigate the cost of creating a design that incorporates the library logo and colors.

b. Other kinds of labels need to be affixed to show ownership or to identify an object. Sometimes a plain papersack can take on special character if an attractive label is affixed to a corner of it.

24. Leaflets

a. Usually a folded sheet of paper that is printed on both sides, making up into a four-page item.

b. This form is often used for programs of a performance or for a general message to a wide-spread audience.

25. Letterheads

a. This has been discussed earlier--it is a printed identification of the library on stationery and used in correspondence.

b. A corresponding envelope goes along.

26. Letters (discussed earlier)

27. Library Cards

a. Use them to the fullest advantage--put hours open and a rundown of major types of materials and services on the back.

b. Make them durable and attractive.

c. Package them in a case that says: "Here Is Your Credit Card to a Lifetime Habit of Growing Intellectually, Emotionally and Socially" or whatever else you think up.

d. Facsimile your special library card into posters and spread them all over to tune people into the value of having one. Advertise the myriad benefits, the least of which is having a valid ID, the best of which is having access to almost every library in the U.S. through interlibrary loan and reciprocal borrowing.

28. Maps

a. Create a map that shows how to get to the library from any place in the area. Note interesting geographical, architectural and historical features along the way.

b. Feature maps in a series
    1) Sites to visit within specified driving distances or by public transport.
    2) Bike routes or jogging paths.
    3) Identification of trees.
    4) Geological mapping of the area.

29. <u>Memorandum</u>

    a. Most often in booklet form, it is useful for stating the library's point of view on a particular subject.

    b. Attractively put together, it is a useful tool of communication with legislators and corporate authorities.

30. <u>Name tags</u>

    a. Those for library personnel have been discussed earlier.

    b. Create an attractive format to be used for program participants, visitors, guests, etc. It is so much more effective than the "HELLO, I'M ..." kind and the difference in cost is minimal for the effect. It's worth investigating. Use the library logo and perhaps tie it in with the design for a label used for mailing.

31. <u>Newsletters</u>

    a. Choose a format that is right for your library:
        1) flat sheet, printed one or two sides
        2) booklet form of several pages stapled in the center
        3) several flat sheets printed front and back stapled in the corner
        4) tabloid, newsprint size

    b. Create a grid, so that you know what will go where in the paper each time (departments). See illustration no. 39

    c. Choose a title, type face and tone in keeping with:
        1) the audience you want to reach
        2) the impact you want to make

    d. Tips for better readership:
        1) Use columns rather than type clear across a page

New Books
Programs
J's, etc.

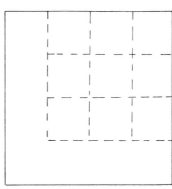

Library – Hours – Phone

39.   Newsletter Grids

        2) Use headlines to capture the content of the story and the reader's interest

      3) Involve the readers, either through guest columns, letters to the editor, an "inquiring reporter" or a system of solicited, signed articles

      4) Change the content as the readership changes--keep in constant touch with the needs and interests of your readers

e. Clearly articulate the purpose of your newsletter and plan the contents accordingly.

      1) annotated listing of new materials on specific topics or in general

      2) descriptions of services

      3) in-depth articles on books or authors

      4) news on library operation and staff notes

      5) library board action

      6) profiles of users

      7) calendar of events

      8) just-for-fun items that pertain to the library (quiz, jumble, puzzle)

      9) selected references to highlight

    10) special sections for categories of users (young readers, antique buffs, arm-chair travelers ...)

f. Date each newsletter and number it if that is of value.

g. Include the pertinent information about the library--name, address, hours open, name of director.

h. Use an attractive layout that makes good use of white space and art.

i. Use a duplicating process that provides a good impression and readability. Do not use photographs unless they print off well.

j. Establish a schedule with deadlines for receipt of material, for printing, for distribution.

k. Establish a distribution plan that is effective and in line with your purpose.

32. Notices

a. They should be designed to create good will even if they remind people of having forgotten something.

b. Some needs for notices:

      1) Expired library card: tell why it is important to renew; find out why they let the card lapse

      2) Library board meetings--time, place, date, agenda; make the meetings worthwhile (plan a program)

      3) Overdue (tardy) books

      4) The book you ordered is in

33. Packets

a. A compilation of materials on a specific topic for a targeted audience.

b. What goes in depends on the purpose.

c. Some ideas:
    1) NEW PARENT PACKET (watch for birth announcements and mail one out)
       --congratulations card or note
       --booklist of parent guides
       --reprints of studies that show the importance of early reading and the example of books in the home
       --booklist of good books to read to the baby
       --pamphlet of nursery rhymes
    2) MY FIRST VISIT TO THE LIBRARY (place in pediatrician offices, apartment complexes, etc., where young children are likely to live)
       --include material for parents and the child
       --in cartoon format tell the library story--from entering the door, to getting a card, to browsing in the children's section, to attending programs, to borrowing materials, to using them at home, to caring for them, to bringing them back and letting someone else enjoy them--include a floor plan with arrows
       --send a bookmark and a put-together-with-parent game
    3) CLASSROOM VISIT PACKET (have something special to give to each child and to leave in the classroom when you go visiting to the school)
    4) FIELD TRIP TO THE LIBRARY (have something for each child to take back to the classroom after the class has visited the library and had a tour and instruction on how to use the public library)
    5) COMMUNITY LEADER PACKET (send this to each new president as the group elects officers--compile helpful data of a general nature regarding how to run a meeting, by-laws writing and revision, fund raising techniques, getting publicity, etc. and include a statement on how the library can help or how all can work together)
    6) LIBRARY VISITOR PACKET (give all visitors a memento of the library--something to take home and show around)
    7) NEW PATRON PACKET (give to all new patrons--you may need different inserts for the Children's Room than for Adult Services) Build it around a specific theme. Include: Calendar of upcoming events and programs; Brochure: "May we introduce, ... Your Library, ... Its Objectives, ... Its Materials, ... Its Services, ... Its Hours, ... Its Location, ... Its Special Advantages Just For You"; Recent Newsletter; Floorplan Map of the Library; Pictorial Guide to Staff Members

34. Pamphlets

    a. Essentially, they are leaflets with many more pages, and cover a topic a bit more thoroughly.

    b. They are especially useful for including in the packets mentioned above.

    c. Commercially produced pamphlets may well serve the needs of most libraries. In any case, a cooperative effort in writing them is a useful route because they are time-consuming to write and design.

35. Placemats

    a. This is a high visibility item if local eating establishments use them over a span of time.

    b. Assistance in paying for this item can come through the sale of ads to local businesses that are not in competition with the restaurant.

    c. Make it very much of a fun thing--the kind that people want to brush the crumbs off and take home as a souvenir.

    d. Be certain that the library's name, address and hours and a few tempting materials and services/programs are mentioned.

36. Postal Meter Messages

Although mentioned before, they are listed here because not only should the library have a message but during a special event, it might be possible to convince one of the big local industries or businesses to catch their usual postal meter message to bring one about the library. It is worth a try, and once established, becomes an annual event.

37. Postcards

Also covered earlier, they deserve being listed in this context, too. They can have a pre-printed message or can serve as an announcement or invitation or notice. To Newcomers: "Welcome to Xtown. How can we help you settle in? Give us a call at (tel. #) or stop by at the Xtown Library and ask for (name)_____." List the address and hours in the blurb.

38. Posters

Sizeable press runs reduce the cost of printed posters. Many exceptionally well designed items are objects of art and deserve recognition as such. Posters in a series can create a great deal of interest. It is worth a staff member's time to keep on top of what is available commercially and what can be printed as a cooperative effort.

39. Programs

    a.   Nice to have for performances in the library and especially valuable for special events such as dedications, corner stone laying ceremonies, etc.

    b.   Contents should include:

        1)   a nice cover that tells a visual story and identifies the event, date, place
        2)   the order of events and the people involved
        3)   data pertinent to the event
        4)   listings of people connected with the event

    c.   Save copies for future reference--in a 100 years it will be significant!

40. Questionnaires

    a.   Ease in answering and returning is the main criterion.

    b.   Design questions that are clear, straightforward and directed to what you want to know. Just a sentence or two of instructions should suffice.

    c.   Pre-test all questionnaires, even those that ask only two questions.

    d.   The form can be as a bookmark or a flat sheet of paper open or folded.

    e.   It is important to have an on-going program of fact-finding that involves library users.

41. Rainchecks

    a.   Pre-printed "coupons" with a place to write in the name of the materials that a patron wants but that isn't available at the time requested.

    b.   It's a psychological ploy, but an effective PR device--at least the person goes away with a promise of getting what s/he wants.

42. Reminders

Essentially the same as "notices."

43. Reports

    a.   Surveys, compilations of evaluations, results of surveys, success stories, challenges to meet--all of these things need to be reported.

b. They should be to the point. Essentially, they are interim points of communication between annual reports.

c. Committee reports were discussed earlier, but they are not necessarily a wide-dissemination report.

d. Some reports can be incorporated into the newsletter and need not be published as a separate publication.

44. <u>Return Card and Return Envelopes</u>

a. Used primarily as an incentive to return questionnaires.

b. The more appealing the design of either, the better the response rate.

c. Design and use either or both in conjunction with another mailing for which a response is important.

45. <u>Self-mailers</u>

Any item that does not need to be placed in an envelope or wrapper to be mailed. It is designed with the idea of being sturdy enough to withstand handling and to incorporate the return address, the addressee and the postage.

46. <u>Signs</u> (refer to Part II and Part VI)

47. <u>Stickers</u>

a. Bumper stickers are like a contagious disease. They are used and they are effective.

b. Lapel stickers are on the rise, with tiny messages that show up on a mass of people to make a point.

c. Lapel stickers have a minimal cost and probably can be far reaching in person-to-person impact.

d. Stickers to affix to telephone directories or to address books, etc., with library hours and telephone number are helpful in spreading the services of the library. Use a clear message.

e. Stickers that young people like to affix to notebooks can be a bit more flippant:

NEED TO KNOW? WANT A GOOD TIME? WHO CARES? WE DO!

CALL_____ CALL_____ CALL_____

48. <u>Supplements</u>

    a. There are times when the library story has to be told straight through to a large audience--thus the newspaper supplement.

    b. These must be designed with care and with a budget source, be it underwritten by a donor or as part of a campaign with funds allocated expressly for this purpose.

    c. Degree of elaborateness depends upon the purpose and budget.

49. <u>Teasers</u>

    a. As inserts in the card catalog, they "speak" to the person who happens upon them. They can say anything from "It's nice to have <u>you</u> in the library" to "SEE our cassette collection for more data on this topic."

    b. Affixed to exits: "Are you leaving satisfied or ... just leaving? Please ask a librarian if you couldn't find what you need."

    c. In all sorts of odd places in the library (go back to the section on signs for a refresher).

50. <u>T-shirts</u>

    a. As one of the biggest items, this is a must. It is a walking advertisement that calls attention to XTown library in a very personal way--to wear a shirt is a testimonial.

    b. Get mileage out of running design contests (with worthwhile prizes).

    c. Custom-made imprinting is available in most areas--check it out as a source of income, too, along with used book sales!

51. <u>Tags</u>

    a. Borrow a popular technique from merchandising and tag certain books or a whole shelf of them as special, hot items to move. People automatically reach for a tagged item as a bargain.

    b. Have fun printing all sorts of messages on red and bright yellow stock: "Yours for the asking," "Enjoy up to three weeks at no cost to you," "If not thoroughly satisfied with this story, try biography or history--you just don't like fiction," "Probably the best buy in town," "Are you getting your money's worth out of this place?"

    c. Run tag days in conjunction with merchandising tag days.

52. <u>Tickets</u>

    a.   Another phenomenon is the ticket craze. People feel better about having a ticket in their hands, even if it's going to be ripped in half or taken away from them.

    b.   Issue tickets for all sorts of library services, materials and programs. Have fun with it.

SUMMING UP

1.   Collect items in each of the categories and learn from comparing.

2.   Use the technique of good design you practised in earlier Parts to create the materials discussed here.

3.   Recognize the myriad of options you have available to communicate.

STEP 43: PREPARING COPY FOR PRINTING.

Accuracy, neatness and pleasing design are essential to the two common kinds of copy: "camera ready" (when you paste down the copy and art work to be photocopies) and copy, art and layout preference for a typesetter and graphic artist to work with and for you to exercise final approval. In either case, the content (copy and art) must fit the space that you have. If the finished product is to have a box of copy 3 inches wide by 4 inches long, determine how many letters (of the type size and style you chose) fit into that 3-inch space and how many lines fit into 4 inches. For example, 15 characters (letters) take up one inch of width. Thus, 15 x 3 = 45. Your typewritten copy must be within that 45-stroke margin (set it at 20 and 65). Six lines of type take up one inch in height. Thus, 6 x 4 = 24. You have 24 lines of 45-character-wide copy. Art will have to be reduced or enlarged to fit its space within the framework of "that which happens to width will also happen to height." For example: a photo that is 4 inches by 8 inches can be reduced 50 percent into a 2" x 4" space but not into a 2" x 3" space.

INTERMISSION: A PAUSE TO REFLECT

HOW DO YOU KNOW HOW EFFECTIVE
YOUR EFFORTS ARE?

How do you measure whether the time and money you are putting into PR are producing commensurate results? In libraries, it is somewhat more difficult to measure results than it is in retailing, but you can establish certain check points and thus gain a relative computation.

1. There are two basic kinds of promotion: a) Immediate Response --you advertise a program for a certain date, time and place; people either come or they don't come. In either case, you still have to figure out how much was due to advertising, how much to the topic, to the date, time, place, weather, or other local conditions, such as competing against a big sporting event (not really advisable) or a popular TV program. b) Attitude (Image) Promotion--you initiate an ongoing campaign of attracting and maintaining users from a segment of the population that previously did not use the library. You start out with a big promotion, but you can't measure results right away because part of your objective is to maintain. Thus, you won't know how successful your plan is until a year or two afterwards. But even then, you have to consider other factors--was it the promotion or the materials and services you built up; was there a strong economic or social reason that prompted library use or that detracted from it?

2. You have to state specifically, at the outset, what it is that you want to measure: a) Increase in circulation of materials. Specify which materials. b) Increase in telephone reference use. c) Increase in productivity (divide the total cost of the budget by the total number of transactions for year 19 __; compare that figure with what you get after you have run a promotional to attract more users).

3. You have to be willing to keep records that will give you clues and concrete evidence of success or failure: a) Right after a staff member has provided a program for a civic club how many people from that group actually come in? How can you find out? Should you put out a "guest book" for everyone entering to sign for that month, or should you give out coupons at the meeting, to be redeemed for some item when they are turned in at the library, or should you just ask club members to come to the library and identify themselves as belonging to X Club? b) You have arranged with a manufacturing company to provide you with space in their employee' newsletter to boost the library. How can you find out how many employees took your invitation to come to the library to heart and really showed up?

c) Following a library program, do people just turn around and leave or do they browse and borrow at the library? d) Can you work with a local high school class to conduct an in-library study right after a big media campaign about general and special library services? (Ask 3 or 4 questions--(1) Did you come to the library to find a specific item? (2) Did you find it? (3) Did you find anything else that interested you? (4) Do you plan to come to the library again?)

     4. You have to analyze high and low response items, be they programs, services, materials, days of the week, hours of the day or whatever. Try to determine a pattern--what's a winning combination, what's a losing one?

     5. You have to combine advertising with publicity through creative thinking. Be the first agency in the area to show interest in the newborn child; be the best source of menu data, be it for 365 dinners, packed lunches or the special holiday events when 30 people come for a buffet luncheon; be the place in town where "being carded" is a positive action. Get a word-of-mouth reputation, a good rapport with business and industry and a steady "in" with local media. Knowing that every year you lose patrons out of natural attrition, just to stay even you have to attract new readers and users, you will seek new ways to keep the library before the public.

     6. You need to borrow a page (or two) from business advertising to adapt to your own local library situation.

     7. You need to devise some way of getting input from your patrons to find out what they like or don't like about the library operation and how they would make it better. Circulate among your users, listen to what they say.

     8. You need to be a good citizen--as a library and as a private person--and be part of civic give-and-take. Does anyone ever ask the librarian to serve or the library to participate? You can determine how much the civic leaders of a community think of you and the library by the amount of contact they have with you. Are visiting dignitaries brought to the library as a matter of course or are you by-passed, only to read about it in the papers after the group has been and gone?

     9. You need to recognize what motivates people in your community to use the library and keep building on your reputation. Never lose track of what the people need, want and benefit from. Measure your return-- once in, do people come back? If you want 99 percent return, find out what you need to do to get it.

     10. The basic rule of thumb in advertising is that you have to plan a campaign for every three months to maintain interest and attract new users to any materials or services. Thus, you should have an on-going, targeted plan for every aspect of the library. If you want to know how to measure success, plan for it. If you want to fail, do things slip-shod. a) List all the materials, services and programs that need advertising and publicity.

b) Get a blank calendar for the year.   c) Check the community calendar, Chase's Calendar of Special Days and Events and any other pertinent calendar for your area.   d) In three-month blocks, figure out what form (a) fits best with items in (c) and pencil in a plan on the blank calendar.   e) Read on, to perfect those advertising skills you have started to build!

PART IX: THE NEWS (MASS) MEDIA

INTRODUCTION

"Media" means radio, television, newspapers and news magazines. "News," loosely defined, is that which is a matter of interest to those people who tune in, turn on, and read. For librarians, the materials include: a) <u>announcements</u> of upcoming events; <u>coverage</u> of events in action; <u>reports</u> of events after they have taken place. b) <u>features</u> (written or pictorial) of specific materials, services, events, or people connected with the library. c) <u>legal notices,</u> as required by law for tax-supported institutions. d) <u>editorial comment</u> (as a direct essay, a letter to the editor, a column or thorough background data supplied to a reporter). e) <u>analysis or review</u> (usually in connection with the annual report, candidates for election to the library board, revenue matters).

It is fact that a good-sized audience can be reached through the news media. It has also been established that it takes a conscious effort "to get into the news (mass) media." You must know the essentials of preparing and placing releases. You must work hard at establishing and maintaining good working relations with editors, reporters, program directors and producers. You must become a master of timing so as to get maximum coverage by meeting deadlines. You must carefully assess the audiences to whom you are directing your releases. You must coordinate the library's news media program through one office so one person is responsible. For most libraries, releases are of a local nature (as opposed to national coverage).

STEP 44: THE NEWSPAPER

1. Find out all you can about each local newspaper (those that publish daily, weekly, etc.). At the top of a sheet of paper write down the name of the newspaper. Then note the answers to the questions asked below:

   a. Read several issues of each paper:
      1) What kind of local news is printed? Make a list of the groups and tax-supported bodies mentioned. What is the style of writing? (<u>Inverted triangle</u>, with all of the essential data in the first sentence and points of diminishing importance in each paragraph that follows; <u>Rectangle,</u> with a short first sentence that "hooks" the reader and with points of essential data following in short

(cont. on p. 117)

NEWSPAPER RESOURCE SHEET

Name of newspaper_____ Office Address_____

Mailing address_____ Zip_____ Tel._____

Publication Schedule_____

Department		
Editor		
Ext. #		
Best to call at		
Copy Deadline		
Stories they like to cover		
How far in advance to notify		

Is there a regular column you could create or contribute to?_____

What are the guidelines?_____

What is the policy regarding photographs?_____

FORM FOR COPY YOU SEND IN:
Margins: L_____ R_____ TOP_____ BOTTOM_____

Page 1: Sample heading:_____
 Spacing:
 _____   _____
 _____   _____
                         _____

Following pages: Sample heading:_____
                                _____

Symbols: To continue story:_____ To end story:_____
Style for:
 Numbers_____ Names, Titles_____
 Dates,Days, Months_____ Paragraphing_____
 Street Addresses_____ Tel. nos._____

Date of visit_____ Name of Library Staff Member_____

Thank you note sent to:_____ on _____

SURVEY OF NEWSPAPER MATERIAL SUBMITTED -- YEAR _____

Name of newspaper _____

STORY	RELEASE DATE	NEWSPAPER DEPT. SENT TO:	DATE SENT	PUBLISHED DATE	EDITION	PAGE #	COLUMN INCHES	PHOTOS	CLIPPING FILED

paragraphs until all of the w's--what, where, who, when, why and how--are disclosed; Mixture, some stories of each way. Pick out a news story of an upcoming event. Can you fit a library story into that format? Try it, substituting your data for the name of the event, the date, the time, the place, the people involved and other details.

2) What kinds of local feature items are published? Make a list. What is the style of writing? Pick out a feature story. Repeat the exercise above, substituting library material to create your own unique copy (newspaper jargon for "manuscript").

3) Make a list of the departments within the paper. Are there some that appear only on certain days (e.g., sports, women's, farm, gardening, children's, teen-age, business, entertainment ...)? List the name of the editor of each department.

Name of newspaper _____

DEPARTMENT	EDITOR	DAYS PUBLISHED	KINDS OF STORIES USED

4) What kinds of photos are printed? Are they taken by a newspaper photographer?

5) Are most articles signed by a newspaper reporter? List the names.

6) What kind of readership does the newspaper pitch to? (You can tell by noting the choice of words, length of sentences, material published, slant of the stories, choice of headlines, editorials, departments, columnists.)

7) Make a list of about a half-dozen things that seem appealing (that you like) about the newspaper.

8) In keeping with what you have just learned about each paper, make a list of newsworthy items in your library for each paper. Don't overlook specific groups of people, and don't just stick to the news department--keep asking yourself--"What have we got in our library that readers of X department would find interesting?"

Newsworthy item	Good for: newspaper/department	kind of story

9) Make a list of the editors you want to contact (for smaller newspapers there is usually an editor-in-chief who handles everything). Look up the telephone numbers. Call them for an appointment to come to the newspaper office to meet them and

talk about how you can work together. (Early afternoon is usually a good time to call editors of daily newspapers. The day after that week's issue has come out is usually best for the editor of a weekly newspaper.)

b. The interview is a time to find out how the editor wants you to send in material, what the deadlines are, what the specific requirements and guidelines are, how much coverage you can expect, what taboos exist. If a "Style Manual" is available, ask for one for the library's reserve section. It will be useful for patrons, too. If you want reporters/photographers to cover events or write a series, find out how far in advance the editor needs details about the time, date and place so he/she can schedule newspaper staff members.

   1) Take the list from no. 8 above. The editor will tell you if your ideas are on base or not. He/she might make alternative suggestions.

   2) Make as many copies as you need of the NEWSPAPER RESOURCE SHEET and the SURVEY sheet (pages 115 and 116). Fill in one for each newspaper during the interviews.

   3) Remember to send a friendly "thank you" note following the interview.

2. Essentials of good newspaper copy:

  a. Content
   1) Is the news really news?
   2) Is all of the necessary information included (who, what, where, when, why, how)? Did you double-check for accuracy of fact and spelling?
   3) Is the release of value to the library--will it help?
   4) Can the average reader understand what you have written (if you use technical terms are they explained)?

  b. Style and Structure
   1) Is the lead good enough to catch and hold attention?
   2) Supply just the facts--a program (not a cute program); a speaker (not an entertaining speaker); a meeting (not a meeting to end all meetings).
   3) Does the body of the story support the lead and keep the reader interested and informed?
   4) Is it clear by the contents what kind of a story it is--news, feature?

  c. Mechanics
   1) Is it clearly typed (be certain the ribbon is clear and dark and the type is clean), double-spaced, with wide margins, on library letterhead, each page number marked, the word "more" written at the bottom of a page if copy continues to the next page, end of story indicated and name of source and release date included?

2) Is there space above the story for the editor to write the head-line and other office instructions? (The heading that you type, giving the name of the newspaper(s) to whom you are sending the release, your name, a brief descriptive line on what the release is about and the release date, appears directly under the letterhead. The copy itself begins half-way down the page.) Follow the instructions for each newspaper's heading and spac-ing style.

3) Is it getting to the editor on time for your release date?

4) Indicate if a story is an "exclusive" or a general release to everyone.

5) Keep a copy of everything you send out. Develop a filing sys-tem for easy retrieval (by date or by subject, etc.)

3. Essentials of good newspaper coverage of a library event:

a. The initial contact
1) Give the editor ample time to schedule a reporter/photographer by sending exact information of date, time, place and type of event. If you ever have an EXTRA! EXTRA! type of occurrence, the paper will respond because it is good business for them to do so.
2) Give the editor clear and pertinent background data.
3) Ask if anything special is needed (telephones, electrical outlets, typewriters ...).

b. At the event
1) Have someone knowledgeable on the facts on hand to greet the reporter/photographer and to assist if and when needed.
2) Have the necessary materials (program, agenda, prepared speeches, etc.) and equipment (as per their request) available.

c. Follow up
1) Have someone available to answer questions if the reporter needs to fill in gaps or verify data after he/she is back at the news-paper office.
2) Check the published story for accuracy. If there are errors, determine what led to them. Ask the editor (reporter) for corrections.
3) Say "thank you."

4. The follow-up:
a. Keep a clipping file (see page 116, "Survey) and post published materials on a bulletin board so patrons and staff can read them. Annotate each clipping with date, page and publication.

b. If a story you send doesn't get in, find out why, in a very friendly manner. It could be your fault, for any of the reasons above under "Essentials of good copy." Correct anything you are doing wrong. Keep at it.

c. If a reporter doesn't show up to cover an event, make an immediate contact. If no one can come, provide for an alternative way to cover and still get a story.

d. Keep updating your "Resource Sheet." Editors have a habit of moving around so you need to keep in touch with who is where.

e. Don't be afraid to express appreciation. Be specific in your note: "Thanks to the help of your newspaper, sixty people came to our program this afternoon. That's a record number, so I thought you should know"; "It is now three months since you ran the feature on our new games and toys department but people are still coming in and saying, 'I read in the paper that you're loaning out toys and games.' This certainly proves that people remember what they read and eventually get around to doing something about an item that especially interests them. You folks deserve a hearty thank-you for the help you have given us in getting out the word."

f. Watch for style and readership changes in a newspaper over a span of time. Grow with the medium to make your message fit.

g. Check within your library to be sure no department is slighted.

h. Do your columns continue to attract a readership?

5. Consider the unusual:

a. Supply the newspaper with library related fillers to use in place of those canned gems we all read (instead of "The highest mountain in ..." let the readers discover "Xtown Public library began in 1806 with 25 books and 12 subscribers ...")

b. Supplement the telephone reference service with a "Newspaper Reference Service" (shades of Heloise, Abby, et al.: "Dear Library,").

c. Plug into the "freebie" books that newspapers get to review and turn that into a library bonanza by having someone on your staff read and review them.

d. Do a lot with local authors, artists, film makers, game/toy designers, and those passing through to promo their works by making the library the place that all these events take place. Turn them into media events.

e. Keep track of facts--if they are significant (newsworthy) turn them into a story--circulation, acquisitions, library card holders, etc.

f. Don't overlook contact with grade and high school (or college) newspapers in your area. Keep in contact with their editors. Feed them stories for their readership. Promote interest and good will.

6. Don't overlook the ordinary:

   a. If a reporter regularly covers the "library beat" don't take him/her for granted. Be on hand to spell names, identify people, etc. Be sure he/she gets advance copies of mailings (minutes, reports). Allow time for interviewing and photographing to take place. Allow the reporter to have "breathing room" but don't neglect him/her.

   b. Tie-in with things that are happening locally. If the local Chamber of Commerce is pushing the municipality's cultural image, suggest that the newspaper do a spread on the library. If a recording star is appearing at the county fair, get her/him to autograph the library's copies of the discs and make a media event of it. Special weeks that always get coverage (National Secretary Week, National Safety Week ...) can stretch over to the library's materials on that topic. If a new film or a TV series is hot, push the book(s) that generated the adaptation.

   c. Offer a blanket invitation to photographers or photojournalists to visit the library at any time. A good photographer will capture the library as it really is--people, in unposed photos, tell a story worth noting by you as well as the public. Knowing that any aspect of the library can be frozen in time and space through a photograph helps you and the rest of the library staff become just a bit more attentive to spider webs in corners and other matters.

7. Co-ordinating the Library's News Media Program:

   a. One person should be in charge of contact with the media. Have all data sheets and inquiries from the media directed to that person.

   b. The News Media Coordinator (Public Information Officer, or whatever the title) should be the one to verify, write and send out the releases, to make arrangements for coverage or interviews, to keep the files for contacts up to date and to be in charge of follow up.

   c. Make copies of the data forms on pages 122, 123, 124 and 125. Use a different color paper for each form. Give several of each to every staff member to use in gathering all the facts for each story. Use the space at the bottom of the sheets to keep tabs and to report back to the source what happened to the story.

   d. If a department is never heard from, find out why. At times, the coordinator may have to be an initiator.

8. Basic principles to follow for good relationships with all media:

   a. Be honest, fair and accurate in giving information for "bad" as well as "good" news.

(cont. on p. 126)

date___/___/___/

LIBRARY NEWS DATA FORM FOR USE WITH ALL MEDIA

TOPIC (can be one or a combination of):

SERVICES _____

MATERIALS _____

PERSONS _____

ACTION TAKEN _____

STATISTIC(S) _____

OTHER _____

WHY THIS IS NEWS ("news peg") _____

_____

_____

ESSENTIAL INFORMATION _____

_____

_____

_____

_____

_____

_____

_____

_____

_____

_____

_____

PICTORIAL POSSIBILITIES _____

_____

_____

_____

_____

SOURCE OF DATA _____LIBRARY DEPT._____TEL.___

TO BE RELEASED TO:_____

TO BE RELEASED ON:_____

OFFICE RECORDS: Data received on:_____Data verified by:_____

Release attached:_____; story not used because _____

_____

Alternate use:_____

_____

DATE___/___/__

LIBRARY EVENT DATA FORM FOR USE WITH ALL MEDIA

VERIFICATION CK

NAME OF EVENT_____

DATE OF EVENT_____

TIME OF EVENT_____

PLACE OF EVENT_____

PEOPLE INVOLVED:
NAME_____ POSITION/TITLE BASIC BACKGROUND INFORMATION_____

_____ _____ _____

_____ _____ _____

_____ _____ _____

_____ _____ _____

_____ _____ _____

DESCRIPTION OF EVENT_____

_____

_____

_____

_____

_____

PICTORIAL POSSIBILITIES_____

_____

FOR WHOM IS THE EVENT?_____

REGISTRATION PROCEDURE?_____COST$_____

_____DUE BY?_____

OTHER DETAILS_____

_____

SOURCE OF DATA_____LIBRARY DEPT._____TEL.____

TO BE RELEASED TO:_____

TO BE RELEASED ON:_____

office records: Data received on:_____ Data verified by:_____
release attached   ::story not used because

DATE ___/___/___

RECAP OF EVENT FORM

verification check

NAME OF EVENT _____

BRIEF DESCRIPTION OF EVENT _____

_____

NAMES OF WINNERS/DEPARTMENT	PRIZE	REASON FOR WINNING

WHAT HAPPENED?_____

WHO CAME? _____

_____

_____

_____

PERTINENT INFORMATION ABOUT THE EVENT THAT SHOULD BE SHARED IN AN ARTICLE:

_____

_____

_____

_____

_____

PHOTOGRAPHS, WITH IDENTIFICATIONS (sheet of paper taped to back of photo),

ARE ATTACHED: ___ (YES) ___(NO)

   Photo credits: _____

_____

SOURCE OF DATA: _____

DEPARTMENT or COMMITTEE: _____

 NAMES OF PEOPLE: _____

TO BE RELEASED TO: _____

TO BE RELEASED ON: _____

LIBRARY FEATURE DATA FORM FOR USE WITH ALL MEDIA

VERIFICATION CK

TOPIC OF FEATURE_____

REASON FOR THE FEATURE(POINTS TO MAKE)_____

_____

_____

ESSENTIAL INFORMATION_____

_____

_____

_____

_____

_____

_____

_____

_____

_____

_____

_____

_____

_____

_____

_____

_____

PICTORIAL POSSIBILITIES:_____

SOURCE OF DATA_____LIBRARY DEPT._____TEL._____

TO BE RELEASED TO:_____

TO BE RELEASED ON:_____

office records: Data received on:_____data verified by:_____

release attached:_____ ::story not used because_____

b. Treat all media equally, respecting the deadlines for each.

c. Say only that which you want to have quoted.

d. Give compliments for good coverage. Inquire politely why, when the library gets left out.

e. Do your homework. Have all of the facts on hand before releasing a story. Provide comparative and background data to help the reporter assess the importance and significance of the story. Anticipate the needs of a reporter.

STEP 45: RADIO

1. Find out all you can about each radio station that people in your service area listen to. (It will take longer to really know the radio fare than it did to gain familiarity with the newspapers. You may have to listen while you're at the library as well as during off hours.)

a. The local newspaper(s) usually publish a section giving the stations and what the daily programs are in time segments. At the top of a sheet of paper write down the call letters and band (numbers on the AM or FM dial). Study the "radio log" to get answers to the following:
1) To what kind of audience does each station cater? (You can tell by the programming emphasis: General, News, Country Western, Disco, Jazz, Rock, Classical, Educational.)
2) Is there a special local news slot? At what time(s)?
3) Is there a talk-show with: (a) in-studio guests; (b) telephone call-ins by listeners; (c) telephone interview between guest and radio host. List the days and times.
4) Is there a "matters of opinion" slot? List days and times.
5) Is there a local "documentary" slot? List days and times.
6) Is there a local "Bulletin Board" slot? List days and times.
7) Are there special departments (farm, home-making, children's ...)? List the days and times they are aired.
8) Is there a booktalk slot or a review of books? List days and times.

b. Spot listen to each station. (If you skip over the network programs and concentrate on local programs--often sustaining or public service in nature--you'll have a better grasp of what is open for libraries.)
1) Do you hear any public service announcements (PSA's)? (These are usually 30 or 60 seconds long and advertise non-profit organizations or events that these groups sponsor.) What are these PSA's? List the groups. Do the PSA's compare favorably with the paid advertising? Do you remember the message? Do you feel persuaded? At what times are PSA's aired? (Before and after what regularly slated programs? Who would be hearing

them because of tuning in?) Could you fill up a half minute or a minute with a "commercial" (PSA) for the library? Try it. Write down a persuasive, informative message.

2) What is the content of local news coverage? Is it heavy on: accidents, tragedies, sensational items, local government, local personalities, local sports, local school events? Is there "on-the-spot" coverage? How long is each story? ($\frac{1}{2}$ minute, 2 minutes, 3 minutes) What do you recall being said? Could you supply a news item about the library? Try it. Write down the facts for the announcer.

3) What is the format of each talk show? Did the host seem "out to get" the guests? Was it a relaxed, chatty session with the host asking and the guest answering? Is there a topic you could discuss on such a show? Jot down a few ideas that would work for the library.

4) What names do you begin to recognize as radio regulars? List them.

5) What do you like about the station's programming? List a few items.

6) As you listen, can you find slots where library news and features would fit in? Make a note of these ideas, keeping in mind the special interests of the audience for each station.

LIBRARY ITEM	GOOD FOR: STATION/ PROGRAM	NAME OF PERSONALITY	DAY	TIME

2. Call the radio station. Ask for the name of the Program Director (write it down) and ask to speak with him/her. Identify yourself. Ask for an appointment time to come to the station to meet with him/her and to learn how you can best share library news. Ask for a tour and a chance to meet the news director, the public service programs director and any other personality who caught your attention and with whom you feel you could work.

   a. These visits are a time for you to find out how, when, where each radio station likes to receive material, to whom each item should be sent (or directed), how stories are edited for a listening audience, how features and guests are chosen, what items are taboo. If this is your first visit, ask to see the operation. (Is there some way you can coordinate a program, display, exhibit ... in the library to share your new-found expertise?)

   b. Take the list from no. 6 above. Talk it over with the program director. He/she will tell you what will or won't work and how you can get the best radio coverage. Make notes.

(cont. on p. 130)

SURVEY OF RADIO and TV MATERIAL SUBMITTED -- YEAR _____

Name of Station _____

ITEM	RELEASE DATE:	DEPT. SENT TO:	DATE SENT	AIRED: DATE	TIME	(VISUALS)	COMMENTS

RADIO RESOURCE SHEET

Name of station
 (call letters)_____ Office
                                          Address_____

Band: AM_____ FM_____

Mailing Address_____ Zip_____ Tel._____

Airing Schedule_____

Department			
Director			
Ext. # Best to call at			
Copy Deadline			
Stories they like to cover			
How far in advance to notify			

Is there a program you could appear on or contribute to?_____

_____

What are the guidelines?_____

_____

What is their interview policy?_____

What is their "matters of opinion" policy?_____

FORM FOR COPY YOU SEND IN:
Margins: L_____ R_____ TOP_____ BOTTOM_____

Page 1: Sample heading:_____

 Spacing: _____

_____ _____

_____ _____

Following pages: Sample Heading:_____

Symbols: To continue story:_____ To end story:_____
Style for:
 Numbers_____ Names, Titles_____

 Dates, Days,Months_____ Paragraphing_____

 Street Addresses_____ Tel. nos._____

Date of visit_____ Name of Library Staff Member_____

Thank you note sent to_____ on_____

c.   Make as many copies as you need for each station of the "News,"
     "Interview" and "PSA" resource sheets for radio stations on pages
     128 and 135.   Fill in one of each for each station during the visit.

d.   Ask for specific guidelines and examples of how each station must
     receive material (requirements vary from station to station so you
     must keep careful notes and update them from time to time be-
     cause changes occur).   Ask for a sample copy of a good radio
     release, a good PSA.   Study them.

e.   Ask about setting up a special slot for library news, events, fea-
     tures.   Set specific guidelines and personalities.   Conclude a for-
     mal agreement now or later, but get the specifics down on paper
     so everyone knows where to be when with what.

f.   Ask about locally produced PSA's and about those packaged by ALA
     and other sources.   With whom would you work? When would they
     be aired? Who would be listening?

g.   Ask about library personnel (staff and board) appearing on talk
     shows.   What makes a good guest? What makes a good topic? Who
     would be listening?

h.   After you get back to the library remember to practise your new-
     found skill in letter-writing and send a hearty "thank you" note.

3.   Essentials of good radio copy:

a.   Content
     1)   Go with the kind of copy that is right for the audience.   For
          radio, write for the speaker (announcer) who communicates to
          the listener.   Make your story clear, brief, memorable.
     2)   The same story must be told in fewer words for radio than for
          newspaper.   You can send the same release to all media if the
          lead (first) paragraph contains all of the essential information.
          The copy editor may re-write your basic data to fit into the
          format of that station's programming but the announcer may
          have to read your story without having seen it before.
     3)   Re-read the message--aloud.   Time it.   Cut out all unnecessary
          words.   Restructure sentences for clarity.
     4)   The same points hold true here as they did for newspaper copy.
          Check back to page 118.

b.   Style and Structure
     1)   Will the announcer be able to read each word, in sequence,
          meaningfully? Avoid jargon, unfamiliar words and foreign
          phrases.   If the pronunciation of a name is difficult, spell it
          out phonetically, in parentheses: Rita Kohn (KÄHN) and Krysta
          (KRIS´ta) Tepper.
     2)   Is the message completely clear? The listener can't go back to

pick up a point--"now you hear it, now you don't" is the radio rule.
3) Keep sentences short.

c. Mechanics
1) If possible, keep a story to one page. Carefully identify succeeding pages.
2) Using library letterhead, clearly type, double-space and allow wide margins.
3) Give a source for the station to contact in case of a question.
4) Specify the release date and time.
5) Get the copy to the right person in sufficient time for the slot in which it is to be used.
6) Always adhere to the guidelines specified by that station.

4. Essentials of good radio public service announcements (PSA's)*:

a. Content
1) A PSA is a carefully constructed message, usually no more than 60 seconds in length, that suffinctly provides the public with information about specific or general materials, services and programs of your library. PSA's are aired at various times during the broadcast day at the discretion of a radio (or television) station manager. A PSA is not a news release, a paid ad, an interview or an ongoing program.
2) You must know exactly what point(s) you wish to make through each specific PSA. Your objectives will determine how you say what (tone).
3) "Sell" items that are of interest to that particular audience. Send a PSA about rock recordings at the library to a rock station, send a PSA about opera recordings at the library to a classical station but send a message about talking book service or an art exhibit to both.
4) Time each PSA to exactly the time length the station specified. Thirty seconds is a shade under but never a breath over thirty seconds.

b. Style and Structure
1) Use short, descriptive, alive words.
2) Use simple, conversational sentences.
3) Start with an attention-getting word or phrase. Give the main message after the listener has had a second to settle in to listening.
4) Repeat the main point of the message at least twice.
5) Read the message to someone else, or tape it. Critique it for content and effect. Re-write, re-read, re-time to get the PSA

---

*Much of the material in this section appeared originally in "PSA Writing" by Rita Kohn; in Prepare!, ed. by Irene Moran. Chicago: ALA, 1978.

<u>exactly</u> right. One word may make the difference between a good and a brilliant PSA.

6) The rule-of-thumb for translating words into seconds is:
10 seconds = 25 words
15 seconds = 37 words
20 seconds = 50 words
30 seconds = 75 words
60 seconds = 150 words

7) Here are some samples:

<u>20 seconds; 50 words</u>

If You've Given Up Reading Because Book Print Is Too Small, Look Again. Your Library Has Best Sellers And Old Favorites In The Large Print Format. And Yes, They're As Light In Weight As Regular Print Books. For Your Reading Pleasure Visit The Public Library For Books In Large Print.

<u>10 seconds: 26 words</u>

Find Out About Books By Mail, A Free Service For People Living In Rural Areas. Register At Your Nearest Public Library And Receive Books By Mail.

<u>15 seconds; 37 words</u>

Enjoy Visiting Museums? Extend The Pleasure To Your Home, At No Cost, By Borrowing Framed Art Reproductions From Your Public Library. Rembrandt, Chagall, Picasso, Winslow Homer And Many Others Are Waiting For You. At Your Public Library.

c. Mechanics

1) Using the station's style preference, type the script clearly. Whether you or someone else tapes the message, the phrasing must be write and every word legible.

2) Type <u>one</u> PSA per page on library letterhead, with a source to contact. Give the beginning and ending airing dates and the number of words and number of seconds. This is a sample set-up, using your letterhead:

(your name)	(event or topic)
(your title)	to be used on ____(day)____,
(extension no.)	(month/date/year)
(date)	through ____(day)____,
	(month/date/year)

PUBLIC SERVICE ANNOUNCEMENT

time: _____seconds
words: _____

THE COPY IS TYPED HERE. USUALLY IN THE STYLE THE STATION PREFERS, ALL UPPER OR UPPER AND LOWER CASE, AND EITHER DOUBLE OR TRIPLE SPACED.

5. Essentials of good radio (live or taped) interviews:

a. Content
1) Have something to say that is of value and interest to that particular audience.

2) Speak as you would to one other person. Be conversational even if you are talking to no one physically present.
3) Know your facts, but don't read--use notes rather than a pre-pared statement.
4) Keep your answers brief, pertinent and within the interest range of the listening audience, but avoid cryptic "yes" and "no" an-swers.
5) Use examples to make a point--make library materials and ser-vices come alive.

b. Style and Structure
1) Speak in your natural voice, don't let the microphone intimidate you.
2) If you're worried about your voice, practise on a tape recorder until you feel relaxed.
3) Avoid irritating mannerisms such as space fillers ("Uh," "You see," "You know what I mean" preceding or following phrases) or clearing your throat or nervous laughter.

c. Mechanics

1) Be on time at the right place with all of the data you need.
2) Keep the data on an easy to get at and easy to read format so as not to shuffle papers or drop things.
3) Avoid wearing clothing or jewelry that rattles, clinks or gets in the way.
4) Stay within the structure of the program--if you have agreed to a specific topic, that's it, but come prepared to fill up the time.
5) Be prepared by knowing your subject and thinking through an interest-catching opening comment and a close that "leaves them wishing for more." Provide the host with pertinent background information.
6) When your session is over, say 'thank you' and leave. Radio personnel are always on a tight schedule.

6. Essentials of good radio coverage at library events:

a. The initial cost
1) Ask the station to cover an event that is clearly of interest to that station's audience. If you know it isn't, but want to cover your bases anyway, send an invitation with specifics of date, time, place, etc., adding that it would be nice to have that station present, but that you clearly understand if they don't feel it is worth their covering.
2) Follow points 3. a. 1) 2) and 3) under Essentials of good news-paper coverage of a library event on page 119.

b. At the event
1) Have someone available to greet and guide each radio reporter. This person should be knowledgeable and capable of giving a radio interview or supplying information.

2) Follow point 3. b. 2) under Essentials of good newspaper coverage of a library event on page 119.

c. Follow-up
1) Have someone available to answer questions if the reporter needs help after he/she returns to the radio station.
2) Check the aired report for accuracy. If there are errors, determine why. Ask for corrections, if necessary.
3) Say thank you.

7. Essentials of good radio programming:
If you and a program director decide on an on-going radio program, be sure to work out all details with a producer. You will need to fill the time with material that captures and keeps listenership. You'll need a distinctive opening and closing that may incorporate music and script. You'll need a format to follow and you'll need some form of monitoring and evaluation for audience reaction. It is wise to have at least five or six programs set before going on the air with a series.

STEP 46: TELEVISION

1. Find out all you can about each TV station that people in your service area watch. (As with radio, plan to take some time to achieve this goal.)

a. The local newspaper(s) usually publish an entertainment section that gives the TV stations and their program offerings. Once again, pull out a clean sheet of paper. At the top, write down the station call letters and channel. Study the "TV Program Guide" (or whatever it is called) to get answers to the following:
1) Is there a special local news program? At what time(s)?
2) Is there a local talk-show with in-studio guests? When?
3) Is there a local "Bulletin Board" to announce events sponsored by non-profit groups? List days and times.
4) Is there a local feature or documentary program? When?

b. Spot listen to each station and take the same inventory that you did for radio stations, but adding the visual dimension. Always think in terms of that camera and what it can do (please, not visual radio!).

2. Call the TV station(s). Follow along as you did for radio, and when you go to visit, take along copies of both the TV RESOURCE SHEET (on page 135) and the PSA RESOURCE SHEET FOR RADIO/TV (on page 136). Learn all that you can about the operation. Work out as many tie-ins that are mutually beneficial to the Station(s) and the Library. Sign them up for an exhibit, a program or give them a permanent spot on the community bulletin board to announce their projects.

(cont. on p. 137)

TV RESOURCE SHEET

Name of station   Office
 (Call letters)_____Address_____

Channel: UHF_____ VHF_____ Cable:_____

Mailing Address_____ Zip_____ Tel._____

Airing Schedule _____

Department		
Producer		
Ext. #		
Best to call at		
Copy Deadline		
Stories they like to cover		
How far in advance to notify		

Is there a program you could appear on or contribute to?_____

_____

What are the guidelines?_____

_____

What is their interview policy?_____

_____

What are the guidelines for copy?_____

_____

_____

_____

_____

Form for copy:
Margins: L_____ R_____ TOP_____ BOTTOM_____

Page 1: Sample Heading:_____

 Spacing: _____

 _____   _____

 _____   _____

Following pages: Sample Heading:_____

Symbols: To continue story:_____ To end story:_____

What are the guidelines for visuals?_____

_____

_____

Date of visit_____Name of Library Staff Member_____

Thank you note sent to_____on_____

PSA RESOURCE SHEET: RADIO/TV

(Call Letters)   Office
Name of Station:_____ Address:_____

Band or Channel: _____ Tel:_____

Mailing Address: _____

Contact(s): NAMES _____ _____ _____

           TITLES _____ _____ _____

           EXT. #s _____ _____ _____
           HOURS BEST
           REACHED _____ _____ _____

PSA requirements: Length: _____seconds _____words

           Airing schedule_____

           Day due in advance of airing_____

           Taboos_____

           Format: Size of paper:_____ Size of card:_____

                   Type all caps:_____ Type u/l case:_____

                   Double space :_____ Triple space:____ Margins:L____ R____

           Visuals: Slides_____ Prints_____ Videotape_____

                    Size _____ Vertical_____ Horizontal_____

                    Cropping_____ Mounting_____

                    Identifying _____

                    Numbering _____

                    Charts _____

                    Lettering _____

           Script specifics _____

           _____

Taping/production schedule _____

Airing format _____

Pick-up schedule _____

Audience reaction studies _____

_____

_____

_____

Notes: _____

_____

_____

Date of visit: _____ Name of Library Staff Member _____

                                _____

   Names of key station people _____ _____

                      Position _____ _____

3. Essentials of good TV copy and visuals:

Basically, without a large expenditure of funds, it's hard to supply TV stations with copy and visuals that fit their needs for programming. Stations usually prefer to cover their own stories and control their locally produced programs. During your visit you will need to determine exactly how to work with your local stations.

4. Essentials of good TV PSA's*:

a. Content
   1) Clearly establish your objectives and your audience. Example: You are introducing a new collection of large print books. Do you have a good readership already so that showing several new titles will do the job of bringing people to the library? Or, are you pioneering a new service so that you need to show that large print books are comfortable and timely? The same subject, treated differently, elicits different action from the audience.
   2) Think both visually and orally. You can adapt a radio PSA to TV but you can't use the same for both. From a standpoint of economics, it is far less expensive to create visuals with slides than with in-studio or on-location video-tape. However, you need expertise in photography and you need some basic still-studio equipment including lighting and a fixed camera for shooting straight down on open books. Learn all you need to know about interest-holding subjects, framing, angles, lighting, contrast and focus for TV PSA slides.
   3) For TV, less is better. Make no more than two points, preferably one, per PSA. Make a strong visual impression.

b. Style and Structure
   1) Know if that station needs horizontal or vertical slides, what their requirements are for mounting, identifying, numbering and lettering.
   2) TV copy has to be paced more slowly than radio copy because the viewer has to coordinate two senses--sight and hearing. This means that the ratio of words to seconds changes, and the relationship between audio and visual needs to be established as well. Audio translates as:
      10 seconds = 20 words
      20 seconds = 40 words
      60 seconds = 125 words
      Visuals: 1 slide or photo for every 10 seconds
   3) The audio and visual segments must be coordinated and enhance each other while advancing the message.
   4) Write the copy to fit the slides. Shoot slides that fit the mes-

---

*Much of the material in this section appeared originally in "PSA Writing" by Rita Kohn; in Prepare!, ed. by Irene Moran. Chicago: ALA, 1978.

sage you want to convey.

5) What you say in words should not duplicate what you say or show in a visual. If you letter a message on a slide, let the viewer read that (unless it is an address to write to), while the announcer expands on that message.

6) Timing is of essence, not only in content but in length as well. Adhere precisely to the length the station alloted to you.

7) For TV a visual logo helps establish instantaneous rapport with viewers. Your library logo should be as familiar as those of commercial products. Couple this visual impact with a distinctive music motif that enhances the image.

8) Here's an example:
ASK ABOUT* ... The Large Print Format   Run dates:
NUMBER L-1   from
: 30   to

1. <u>New York Times &</u> <u>Reader's Digest</u>

     Ask about books, newspapers and magazines in the large print format at your public library.

2. Holding magnifying glass
3. Cookbook (open)

     If reading regular print is a strain, you'll find books on all subjects from cookbooks to popular novels.

4. Spine shot of regular and large print, same title

     Simultaneous printing means current materials are available to all readers.

5. Open page shot of regular & large print, same title

     For ease in reading ... Ask about the large print format at your public library or bookmobile stop in the Corn Belt, Rolling Prairie or Lincoln Trail Library systems.

6. LOGOS (RPL, LTLS, CBLS)

c. Mechanics
  1) Follow the same procedure as for radio, adapting the copy, however, to show what words go with which slide (visual).
  2) Number and coordinate each slide precisely. Check and double-check. It's awful having the wrong visual show up.
  3) Deliver the spots on the correct date and at the exact time to the right person at the appointed place.
  4) If you want the visuals back, be sure to specify this and be right there to claim them when the production crew has completed use. Do not expect TV personnel to package and mail your slides after you have received free air time in a very costly operation.
  5) Develop a filing system of slides. Being able to pull a slide from one PSA to use in another is very helpful. Store slides in a safe, dry place.
  6) File scripts for easy retrieval. Some phrases are worth re-using.

---

*Script from the series created as a cooperative project between three library systems in Central Illinois, created by Larry Pepper and Rita Kohn.

7) Never give a station the only slide that you have. It just may get lost. Keep a master file of duplicates. This may be expensive, but it costs less than re-shooting an entire spot.

8) Document when and how the PSA was aired. Use the "SURVEY OF PSA MATERIAL SUBMITTED" sheet to keep track.

9) Consider working with other libraries, exchanging and sharing materials for the benefit of all. This is crucial where one station covers several neighboring communities and a cooperative approach is the only way you can get TV (or in some cases, radio) time.

10) If your area is covered by two or more stations, survey each independently and, if possible, devise a PSA schedule that enables you to alternate materials so as to avoid having to create completely new scripts all the way around. If you do alternate, tell station managers what you are doing.

11) When you are having photographs taken to be used in a PSA, have your subjects sign a "no payment rights" form (that your board formulates) to protect your library from commercial residuals claims by any subject you photograph in good faith for "free". Make it clear to your subject that she/he is freely consenting to pose.

12) If you use "canned" (already prepared materials from a commercial source or from another library, such as ALA spots) PSA's, use the same care as you would if you were producing your own. Screen the material and be sure it is suitable and applicable for your library and for the audience.

13) Follow up with appreciation.

5. Essentials of good TV (live or videotaped) interviews:

   a. Content
      1) Think visually. SHOW and tell. If it is a "sit around the table" interview, bring materials that will catch interest. It might be best to remove plastic protective coverings because they produce glare and lessen the impact of the book jacket.
      2) Show the usual as well as the unusual, assuming that a lot of people who watch TV haven't been inside your library.
      3) Follow the same criteria as for a radio interview. Be natural, be informative without overwhelming. Attempt to make only as many points as viewers can absorb in that time span.
      4) Come prepared with an opening and closing statement and be able to brief the host so that he/she can ask "intelligent" questions.

   b. Style and Structure
      1) Dress appropriately. Some colors of clothing fade out on camera. Ask about this.
      2) Get pointers on good camera angles and eye contact with viewers.
      3) If you plan to read from a teleprompter, practise.
      4) If, for some reason, you have to read a prepared statement from a script, learn how to also have eye contact and not lose your place.

(cont. on p. 141)

SURVEY OF PSA MATERIAL SUBMITTED -- YEAR

DATE	TIME	PLACE TO DELIVER	TOPIC	AIRING SCHEDULE	DATE	TIME	PLACE TO PICK UP	PERSON IN CHARGE

c. Mechanics
1) Follow the same principles as for radio.
2) Always be prepared to fill up the full time. Bring something extra along just in case you got through the prepared agenda a mite faster than you had anticipated.
3) Gather up all of your materials, say "thank you" and leave. Send a note of appreciation after you get back to the library.

6. Essentials of good **TV** coverage at library events:

Follow the same principles as for radio, but remember the space and lighting requirements of **TV** and allow for them. You may also have to schedule events with **TV** news air times in mind. Determine all of these factors <u>before</u> setting up the time and place of the event.

7. Essentials of good **TV** programming:

a. Content
1) Have a definite plan for the program (News-magazine, documentary, feature.)
2) Gear the program for local audience appeal.
3) Be certain that the local station can produce that program.

b. Style and Structure
1) Work this out specifically with the producer of the TV station.
2) Consider the return for the cost. Choose the theme accordingly.

c. Mechanics
1) Recognize the amount of time it takes to put together a TV program of the length you and the station agree upon and arrange your work schedule at the library accordingly.
2) Work cooperatively, if possible, and produce programs that can be shared and re-played.

STEP 47: THE NEWS MAGAZINE.

If a news magazine is published within your area and has a local content and readership, meet with the editor to determine how best to get library coverage. For feature articles, work with free-lance writers and photographers if that is the best route. If there is a local "news in brief" section or a local "calendar of events" determine deadlines and get your data in so that library programs and events are listed. If possible, have the library become a regular department. Establish all guidelines for copy, deadlines and content and assign one person to coordinate the activity.

STEP 48: THE NEWS CONFERENCE

If you call it a press conference, don't expect radio and TV to show up. But, be prepared for some problems if all three kinds of media are invited together.

1. Some basics:
   a. The news conference is a fair way to release a story simultaneously to all media. But don't leak news ahead of time and lose the impact.
   b. Schedule the news conference for good release time for all media.
   c. Create a setting that is as interesting for TV and radio as it is for newspaper.
   d. Call a news conference only if what will be released is worthy of asking all those people to come to you. If the data could just as easily be handled with a routine news release don't schedule a conference.

2. If the message has dramatic impact, is of extreme consequence to a lot of people or is a super-special event, call a news conference:
   a. Introduce a new library director to the community.
   b. Introduce drastic changes in library policy, procedure, budget.
   c. Unveil building plans.
   d. Announce a large bequest, grant or gift.
   e. Unveil a rare find or special collection.

3. How to set up a news conference:
   a. Know exactly why you are holding it.
   b. Set the time, date, place, who is in charge, how long it will take, who is to be present, what data and materials are needed.
   c. Invite the participants and be sure they know why they are present and that they are prepared to speak if a question is directed toward them.
   d. Invite the media representatives. Be fair to all. Give full data and determine if there are special needs.
   e. The equipment you need to provide will depend on the size of the community, who from the media comes and how "hot" the item is (extremely urgent, of national consequence). Standard equipment can include: telephones, typewriters, typing paper, working space, wiring, seating and PA System for speaker and questioners.
   f. Compose the opening statement.
   g. Anticipate probable questions. Have participants from the library who are knowledgeable so that they can respond.
   h. Prepare a news kit with:
      background material
      a copy of the prepared statement
      names and positions of library people involved with the event.
      Make this available at the beginning of the conference and allow for time for the media representatives to look over the material.
   i. Prepare exhibits or demonstrations if either or both are pertinent and helpful.
   j. Allow sufficient time.
   k. Be available for follow-up data if a question arises after a reporter is back at the office.

4. Follow-up:

a. Check on the content of the coverage. If there are errors, find out why and correct them.
b. Say "thank you" to all participants.

PART X: AUDIO-VISUAL PRESENTATION

STEP 49: OVERHEAD TRANSPARENCIES

1. Basic decisions:

    a. What is the purpose and target audience of the program in which the transparency will be used? Examples:
        1) To show the relationship between library income and expenditures to civic groups as part of an informational campaign (use charts, graphs, distribution pies ...)
        2) To preview the floor plan of the library and follow a flow chart of the tour for library visitors.
        3) To show the steps in researching a topic to a junior high class.

    b. How many transparencies should you use during any one presentation? This depends upon the topic, the length of the presentation, the audience and the content of the program.

    c. What needs to be illustrated through transparencies? Carefully scrutinize the presentation outline--what points can best be illustrated with a visual aid that is flashed on a screen so people can study it and not merely rely on the spoken word?

2. Specific points to follow:

    a. Look at already completed transparencies. What is good about them, what is poorly done? Is the lettering too small, is too much crowded into a small space, is the spacing good, are the lines clear and strong, are the colors clear, etc.

    b. It is easier to relate concrete information than abstract ideas with transparencies, however, abstractions can be conveyed through clever use of the medium (an entire story can be drawn on transparencies and retold with oral narration).

    c. Investigate the room in which the program is to be given. Is it a good facility for using an overhead projector? Is the ventilation good? Is there space for the projector, screen and audience with everyone able to see?

    d. Use transparencies to enhance the text, not to repeat it. It is all right to flash the outline of your talk on the overhead projector but

144

unpardonable to have the full script to read along with the audience.

3. Specifics of production:

   a. Plan out on a piece of paper (the exact size of the clear plastic or acetate that you will be using for the final product) exactly what you want to show where on the projection. Good design and clear content are essential.

   b. Use the proper materials: lettering pen, grease pencils, adhesive tape, colored papers for transparencies, cutouts, clear plastic or acetate, dry transfer lettering (depending on what you want to show, you may need ruler, T-square or right-angle triangle, compass, protractor).

   c. Pre-test all transparencies before you actually use them.

   d. Number and correlate each transparency with the right spot in the text.

   e. If desired, mount on a cardboard frame for ease in handling and storage.

   f. Mark the "right side up" to avoid fumbling during the presentation.

   g. Place all transparencies in the order in which they are to be used.

   h. Develop a system of how to slip used transparencies into a container so that they are safe but out of the way during the remainder of the presentation.

   i. Investigate the duplication for transparency capability of your office copier and follow directions.

4. Storage and Retrieval:

   a. Provide for a dry-cool place for storage.

   b. Place cardboard around each transparency as a protective sleeve and keep each in a file-folder that is appropriately labeled.

   c. Store in such a way that you can retrieve what you need to use in a variety of situations. Update facts and figures as the data changes so that you are always ready to provide a talk with the newest information.

5. Develop a budget:

   a. Equipment: overhead projector, screen, storage facilities, copier.

   b. Accessories: clear plastic or acetate, lettering pen, dry transfer lettering, grease pencils, colored adhesive tape, acrylic paint, colored paper, cutouts, ruler, T-square, right-angle triangle, compass, protractor.

    c.   Production costs: staff time, artist, equipment upkeep, copies.

STEP 50: CASSETTE TAPE RECORDING

1. Basic decisions:

    a.   What is the purpose and target audience of the recording? Examples:
        1) The sound track for a general orientation slide show for new patrons.
        2) A friendly message to go with materials sent by courier to nursing homes.
        3) Instructions for on-site use of library equipment.
        4) "Read Alongs" for children to check out with corresponding picture books.
        5) Staff or patron reviews of that week's new books sent to key locations where people have access to tape players (staff rooms of major industries in the community).
        6) Oral history project and documentation of significant local events for preservation of local history.

    b.   How long should the tape recording be? Determine what is the absolute listener-interest time for each audience and what the maximum taping allottment is for any project.

    c.   What do you want to say?
        1) Jot down ideas--develop a theme--set one or two specific goals to be accomplished.
        2) Write a script. Have a beginning, middle and end.
        3) Pre-test and re-write as need be.

    d.   What kind of music (or sound effects), if any, do you want to integrate into the final tape?

    e.   Will you use one voice, two or several?

2. Basic points to follow:

    a.   Listen to professionally produced tapes. Be critical--what is good, what won't work for you?

    b.   Use only quality tape recorders, players and tapes. Do careful market research to find the best equipment within your budget.

    c.   Choose someone with a trained recording voice to do the narration (local radio or TV personalities, speech teacher, drama coach ...).

    d. If you must record on your own, and it's a new experience, get a good feel of the recorder and its capabilities by experimenting a lot:

        1) Speak into the microphone at varying distances while the volume is alternately set at each level.

        2) Say the words "POP," "BUT," "STOP" with the microphone held right up to your mouth. Now say the same words while holding the mike slightly higher, then slightly lower, then farther away from your mouth.

        3) Experiment with different voice pitches that you have.

        4) Follow the tape recorder instructions implicitly and learn how to handle the machine.

3. Specifics of Taping:

    a. The recording location:

        1) Test the recording qualities of any room before using it as the setting for the final tape.

        2) Strive for a rich tone free from distracting sounds (including clocks, muffled voices through a closed door, traffic through a closed window, etc.).

        3) If you don't have access to a recording studio you can create a good sound by draping blankets around the area in which you do record.

    b. The narration:

        1) Practice the script until it's perfect. Then go right through.

        2) Taping oral history is a subject of its own--refer to guides.

        3) Always pre-test the recording level, distance of mike, etc. before making the final recording.

        4) Synchronize with slides if you're making a slide/tape program.

    c. Adding music:

        1) Background music should in no way detract from the spoken word.

        2) Use instrumental music, either tapes or discs in good condition.

        3) Mark the script for the specific volume and sequence of music so that you know when to turn on each element of the music you have chosen.

        4) For a recording with music underplaying, keep the tape or disc running on low volume throughout the narration.

        5) Turn up the music volume when you want to bridge narrative segments and move the mike a bit closer to your mouth for speaking. Turn the music back down after the bridge.

        6) Practice as many times as necessary to make a quality recording.

4. Duplication of tapes--Storage and Retrieval:

    a. It is best to make at least one duplicate and use it instead of the original.

b. Mark each tape carefully. Develop a system that works for you.

c. Catalog the tapes so that you and program-givers know what is available.

d. Store tapes in a cool, safe place, preferably a metal cabinet.

5. Develop a budget:

a. Equipment: tape recorder, player, microphones, tape duplicator, phonograph, storage facilities.

b. Accessories: tapes, extension cords, music recordings (tape or disc).

c. Production costs: staff time, room use, utilities, equipment upkeep.

STEP 51: SLIDE/TAPE SHOW (PRESENTATION)

1. Basic decisions:

a. What is the purpose and target audience of the slide/tape show? Examples:
    1) As a report to the library board regarding the circulation procedure at your library and various other options as photographed at other locations (or any other library operation that needs scrutiny).
    2) As a self-contained program that can travel to malls, fairs, etc. via back-screen projection and automatic sound track synchronization.
    3) As a campaign to interest civic groups in participating in the "Library Volunteers" program.
    4) As an in-service training program for library staff on the essentials of productive communication skills.

b. How long should the presentation be?
    1) Twenty minutes is the suggested optimum length for large group presentation.
    2) Five minutes is a good length for automatic back-screen projection.
    3) A fast-paced ten-minute program is a dynamic opener for group discussion or action.
    4) Basically, use good common sense to achieve the one or two goals that you have set.

c. What do you want to convey?
    1) Follow 1.c. of Step 50 (Cassette tape recording) for the audio part and to develop the "story line."
    2) Depending upon the theme, slides will either be "staged" or "candid." Thus, you must develop the message precisely so

that you know what can best be conveyed through the visuals. (Review the section on PSA's for TV production because much of the rationale applies here.)

    d. Follow 1. d. and 1. e. of Step 50 (Cassette tape recording).

2. Basic points to follow:

    a. Look at slide/tape presentations that are already put together and analyze them critically. What can you learn from them about good production?

    b. Use only quality slides (for candid shots there may not be a choice --you may have to sacrifice quality for content). Throw out those that are too dark, are washed out or have no center of interest.

    c. Weed out extraneous slides, no matter how great the content. If they don't advance the story-line and directly contribute to the achievement of the stated goal, save them for some other time or enlarge them as prints for an advertisement, etc.

    d. Learn how to use the camera to its fullest efficiency or else have someone who knows how to handle a camera work with you to fulfill the precise needs of the script (or outline, depending upon how you are working).

    e. Unless the slide presentation is of a specifically local nature, check with the ALA Public Information Office, your state library association office and your A-V coordinator regarding "canned" (already prepared) presentations that you can rent or borrow at a cost much lower than what it takes to produce one from scratch.

    f. Learn from your local photography shop what film is best to use for indoor or outdoor slides and how much spotlighting is required to get the effect that you need for indoor shots.

    g. For the best projection it is suggested that horizontal shots be used. Vertical slides have a tendency to spill over the top or bottom edges of the screen.

    h. Some colors photograph better than others--this may influence you in some content choices.

    i. Plastic book jackets and glossy photos bounce the light off. You may photograph a blob of light rather than a subject.

    j. Photographing through doors of glass (as in cases) needs special care to avoid reflections and glare. Photograph from an angle rather than straight on.

    k. Examine the full content of a shot through the viewfinder before shooting. Is it too busy? Is there a calendar or a clock that will date the slide so that it has limited use? Remove anything that would be distracting.

l. Is the picture boring? What can you do to make a picture interesting?

m. Is this a picture that will be flashed on and off in a flick? In that case make the impact immediate and strong--don't expect viewers to read signs in a big hurry--unless a jungle of signs is what you want to show.

n. Is this a picture that will stay in view for a full minute? Is there enough content to make it interesting for a group to sit there looking at it?

o. Absolutely coordinate the audio with the visual both in script and in synchronization. Do not describe the picture, but if you are talking about reading to shut-ins, have a slide that shows a volunteer in action.

p. Follow the same word-per-time count as for TV PSA's.

3. Specifics on production:

a. Work from a "story-board" such as the script prepared for the TV PSA (page 138) so that you know what kind of picture goes with what text.

b. Decide on a style that best relates your message and helps achieve the goals you have set--(formal, zany, fantastic, understated, etc.)

c. Plan the opening (title slide) to immediately capture the audience and to convey the tone and the objective. Choose a title that is both creative and accurate. Give the name and status of the agency or person who produced the presentation. The title and other data can be spelled out on one of those signboards you have or can be a photograph of a title poster specifically created with your best poster-making technique. (Look at already prepared slide/tape shows to learn how to handle this part of the operation).

d. After all of the slides are assembled for sorting and viewing, be extremely critical. You may need to discard 2/3 of what you shot and may need to re-take several items.

e. Test your first "completed" show. Are there too many facts? Is there a gap in continuity? Is it dull? Does it miss the mark? Do viewers say, "It's nice, but what's the point?" Go back to the drawing board if you have to. The first time-around may be a disaster. Try again.

f. Load slides in the correct order, in the correct side up, in trays or carousels of the appropriate size. It is accepted practice to label slides in the upper-right-hand corner if they are placed in 80-unit trays and in the upper-left-hand corner if they are placed in 140-unit trays.

g. ALWAYS MAKE DUPLICATES OF SLIDES. Keep one complete set in a safe place and use the other as your program.

h. Follow along Step 50 (Cassette Tape Recording) for the Audio.

i. Read through Step 52 (Film) to get ideas because the rationale is so similar despite the differences in the medium.

j. Plan the closing slide to "wrap it all up" so that the message is reiterated and clear. Learn techniques from the last slides of shows that you view.

k. Be sure to have any people who appear on the slides sign a release form (as for TV PSA's).

4. Storage and Retrieval:

a. Store a show in its entirety with all of the elements packaged together--slides, tapes, script.

b. Label each element separately as to title, length of the total production (in terms of time), and the exact date, location and group to which they were presented. Label the package in which all of the elements are stored.

c. Check all parts after each showing to make sure each element is intact.

d. Develop a filing system to provide for easy and accurate retrieval.

5. Presentation:

a. Always check out the room and the facilities before agreeing to give a slide/tape presentation there. Can it be darkened? Is the line of vision clear?

b. Always check out the equipment--your own and any that is provided on the premises. Be certain everything is in working order.

c. Always carry an extra bulb for the slide projector, an electric cord and an adapter for electrical outlets (many are not three-pronged as are pieces of electrical equipment).

d. Always run through the entire program to be certain slides are in correct order and right-side-up and to be certain that the tape is in good condition and synchronized.

e. Always carry the script for emergencies.

6. Develop a budget:

a. Equipment: 35 mm camera, spotlights (2-4), slide projector, screen (for visuals). Step 50 (Cassette Tape Recording), no. 5 lists the audio needs. Storage facilities. Slide sorter.

b. Accessories: film for slides (color or black and white), carousels or trays, storage boxes, projector bulbs.

c. Production costs: staff time, equipment upkeep, film developing and duplication of slides.

7. Slides with live narration:

a. It may simply be better, for your needs, to develop a slide presentation with you (or whoever it is that is giving the program) speaking. This certainly makes production easier.

b. Use a projector that permits you to advance slides (and focus) with a remote control unit so that you can stay at the front of the audience.

c. Adjust your voice (as you would the volume of the tape) so that you can be heard. If a microphone is best for you, see to it that you have one.

d. Practice for a smooth delivery.

STEP 52: FILM

1. Basic decisions:

a. What is the purpose and target audience of the film? Examples:
   1) To tell the story of two patrons who come to the library--one to get information about building a tree-house (or whatever) and the other to attend a program--and their adventures, as a story-line for a tour of the library and an introduction to its various services and materials.
   2) To tell the story of a book, from order, to arrival, to processing, to shelving, to borrowing, the circumstances in the home it goes to, its return, etc.
   3) To tell the story of a library board member, or a volunteer, over a year's time of activity.

b. What kind of camera should be used?

1) It is best to visit local photography shops and learn from personnel there because the situation changes rapidly.
2) Super 8 cameras are usually easier and less expensive to use than are 16mm movie cameras (the 8mm is basically passé). Always anchor the camera on a tripod.

c. How long should the film be?
1) A lot depends on the purpose and target audience.
2) Ten minutes is a good length for an informational film; fifteen minutes works well for a feature film that involves a lot of action and human interest; twenty minutes provides a good documentary framework.
3) Budget may well determine length.

d. What "style" should the film adopt?
1) The goals that you want to reach will determine whether you make this a straightforward film, a mystery (with broad clues dropped but nothing worked out until the very end), a melodrama, etc.
2) Whatever you decide, be certain that you carry it off throughout.

e. Will you film "people" or use animation?
1) It is technically easier to film people, but if you have the talent and the facilities for animation, you will have a product with greater longevity.
2) The people you work with must follow your directions to "tell the story" as you want it told.
3) Clothing choices must be such that they will neither serve to stereotype nor date the film too much.

2. Basic Points to follow:

a. View a lot of films over and over. What do you like, what do you dislike about each? Make notes about angles, shots, content, story line, sequence, impact.

b. Until you become very adept at editing, plan to shoot the entire film in sequence. This may mean keeping your storyline simple and curtailing the urge to do an outdoors opening scene, an indoors second scene, a third scene in a shopping mall and then back to the outdoors, etc.

c. To make editing easier, leave from one to two seconds of blank film between scenes. (You get blank frames by covering the camera lens and letting the camera run for a count of 1, 2, ...)

d. Expect to re-shoot some scenes. Even the professionals do!

e. As you plan, think through the things that can "date" each scene. Take appropriate steps to eliminate them.

f. Start a new roll of film by shooting two frames of its roll number written on a sheet of paper. Also write the number on each cartridge. Be careful to consecutively number each roll of film correctly.

g. As you shoot a scene, note the film roll number on the script.

DATE	FILM ROLL #	SCENE #	SCRIPT OUTLINE		
			Visual conception	Audio	Stage Directions

h. Make enough copies of the script for everyone involved to have one ahead of time to become familiar with it.

i. Prior to shooting, go over the script with the actors. Talk through the scenes so that they understand the theme and basic objectives and how they must project both.

j. Work for a pleasant projection of the library image.

k. Maintain even lighting throughout the whole film. Different circumstances require different approaches--a brightly lit room may need only two spots* whereas a very shaded or dimly lit area requires four spots.

l. Even if it takes you several days to complete filming, if the script indicates that the action takes place during one block of time (an hour at the library--or a day) have the actors dressed and coiffed the same. Also be certain that furnishings and props remain constant (same vase and same flowers; same books on display, etc.)

m. Be able to pick up each new scene in exact correlation with the one just completed, so note exactly where each actor was placed, what each was doing and how (example: "Actor A": sitting with right hand on table, left hand on lap, etc.)

n. Have actors sign a "no payment rights" form (as in the production of TV PSA's Step 46) to protect your library from future claims. Once again, make it clear to actors that they are freely consenting to appear in the film.

o. Have one person in charge (producer) of the whole operation--purchasing, scheduling, editing and writing the storyline.

---

*Spotlights--lights of high degree of brightness that illuminate a specific area.

p. Develop a "film-making" vocabulary:
1) LIGHTING
    Key lighting = main lights
    Fill lighting = secondary lights
    Lighting intensity = degree of brightness
2) FILM
    Frame = the space of one image on the film
    Blank frames = space on film that has been deliberately ex-
      posed with your hand over the lens
    Correlation of feet of film to time it takes to view it
      for Super 8--50 feet = 2 minutes 30 seconds
                  100 " = 5   "
                  300 " = 15   "
                  400 " = 20   "

3) FILMING
    Full shot = an entire image, such as all of a person or building
      at some distance so that the surroundings are visible
    Medium shot = moving closer in so that you are showing more
      of the subject and less of the surroundings
    Close-up = one particular aspect, such as the face of a person
      or the door of a building so that you see all the features
      clearly
    Tight shot = another term for a close-up
    Pan = moving the camera (slowly) in a left-right or up-down
      direction to give a sweeping view
    Zoom = move in on a subject from a distance to right close in
      (can be done with zoom lens so that the camera and camera-
      person never move)
    Hold = stay on the subject for a count of three or four
    Framing = getting the subject in an aesthetically pleasing view,
      such as a building with a tree overhang and a span of lawn
      with shrubbery
    Angles = the approach, such as from above, from below, from
      the right, from the left or straight on
    Reverse angles = shooting from the back
    Exterior shot = outdoors
    Interior shot = indoors
4) STORY
    Storyline = the theme that runs through the film and is its
      reason for being, as the adventures of a first day at the li-
      brary with a three-year old
    Continuity = keeping the storyline on track for the audio and
      visual segments (not getting sidetracked to show a dog that
      happened to run in because it's cute, but it has nothing to do
      with the story in its original form)
    Scenes = the sequence of the story as it is told from beginning
      to end

Storyboarding = the first conception of the visual and audio sequences created through rough sketches, usually on 5" x 7" cards that are folded in half. On the left-hand side is a sketch of the visual, on the right-hand side of the card are notes for stage directions, captions, dialogue, narration. You use cards so that you can drop ideas in and out and rearrange. You always number the cards in the upper right-hand corner.

40. Story Boards

Straight sequence = going from scene 1 to "the end"

Script = the final copy of the story as put together after altering and rearranging the storyboards (it is on sheets of paper, typed double-spaced, on one side only) and contains the scenes, stage directions, dialogue and narration and a space to note the date it was shot and the number of the roll of film on which it appears.

One page of single space script = 1 to $1\frac{1}{2}$ minutes of screen time. A 15 min. film needs 10-12 pages of single-space or 20-24 pages doublespace.

5) MUSIC

Tempo = degree of fastness or slowness

Up = volume higher to bridge between narration or dialogue

Under = volume down (low) so that it is there but hardly discernible

Instrumental = no voices(s), as a piano or a guitar or an ensemble or band

Vocal = background music with voice singing lyrics

6) PERSONNEL

Producer = the one person in charge, who usually outlays the money

Director = the artistic "incharge" person, who works with the actors and the producer to create a worthwhile product

Musical director = the person who may select and say where each segment of music fits in the total structure

Actors = people who portray the roles in accordance with the script and instructions from the director

Narrator = the voice that tells the story but is not seen

Technicians = the people who set the physical aspects of the scene and see to it that the lighting is correct, that all props are on hand, etc.

Cameraperson = the individual who actually handles the camera and shoots the film in accordance with what directions are given by the director

Editor = the person who looks at all of the rolls of film after they have been developed and who then proceeds to cut it up and put it back together again according to the storyline so that the message is clear to the viewer

7) PRODUCTION

Focus = regarding camera, keeping the subject from being fuzzy (as "Out of Focus"); regarding stage direction, keeping the story-line moving without digressing

Location = the place where the filming will take place

Props = things the actors handle, such as books, puppets, the telephone, etc.

Title = the opening parts of the film that tell its name, who made it, who is in it

Close = the very last scene that gives credits, etc.

3. Basic outline for shooting each scene with live actors:

a. Inspect the location: without film in the camera (or with film but not really shooting), frame each scene. Things may have to be changed between the original conception of the script and the subsequent filming. Re-work the script at this point.

b. Move furniture, props, etc. prior to the actors coming onto location (they should not be kept waiting around).

c. Set up the camera and lights for the angle you want.

d. Talk through the scene with the actors. State the point (what the scene must accomplish) and give precise directions regarding what to do, where to go, how to move.

e. Walk actors through the scene. Make necessary adjustments and changes.

f. Turn the lights on and walk the actors through the scene, following along through the camera but not shooting. Be especially careful about shadows due to improper placement of spots or poor planning of placement of people and objects.

g. Shoot the scene through, stopping only if necessary and then picking up where you left off. Identify the scene by shooting a frame of its number written on cardboard held up by someone.

h. Clear away equipment, unless you are set up in a studio where no one will damage or walk off with anything.

4. How to handle the camera:

a. Use SLOW movement--do not jerk the camera--for panning.

b. Mostly, shoot straight on (especially signs).

c. To show rapid change, shoot $\frac{1}{2}$-second frames while adding or re-moving elements (books "going like hotcakes")

d. MEASURE DISTANCE for exact focus in accordance with your camera:

X subject   Make up a chart:

O camera <u>lens</u>

____ ft = close up
____ ft = full shot
____ ft = tight shot
____ ft = medium shot
____ ft = pan shot

5. How to create title and credits:

a. These must go along with the theme and fit into the setting and style of the location.

b. Use your best sign-making talents and shoot straight on, framing as needed.

<u>at the opening</u>   <u>at the end</u>
THE SUCCESS OF SECRETS ACKNOWLEDGMENTS
 produced by the
 Reference Dpt.
of the XTOWN LIBRARY
 directed by
 CECIL D. HILL
 starring the
High School Archeology THE
  Club   END

One trick is to paste lettering on clear plastic and shoot through it to a background. (It looks like you have lettered the stacks or people milling about.)

6. How to use spot lights.   This is a possible set-up.

spot #3   spot #4

   SUBJECT
   FRAME

spot #1   spot #2
   camera

The approach for you to use is to talk with your local photography shop and learn what is best regarding your specific situation.   That's a nice way of getting these people involved in a very functional manner.

7. How to write a script:

   a. Tell a straightforward story.

   b. Keep the objective and the theme in mind at all times, as you develop the visual action and the audio narration or dialogue.

   c. Start out with an outline or a few paragraphs that describe what you want an audience to experience via a movie camera.

   d. Then gather details--to accomplish goal "a," what must you show and tell?

   e. Evaluate the mass of details--is it too much? What can you eliminate? Is the goal too broad? Is it too thin? What needs to be added to make it more interesting?

   f. Then move to the 5" x 7" cards and mix and match them until you have a sequence that looks good to you and a few others you ask to test it out. Make changes and put it all together on typing paper, being certain that you have people on hand to "take the parts" you have created.

   g. Spend a lot of time in this planning stage. The tighter the storyline the more interesting the film will be.

   h. Think through all the directing techniques you will need to employ and incorporate them into the script.

   i. You really are using the form of film scripts used by television and motion picture directors. Here is a possible script, used more for the form than the content in this case:

      LONG SHOT of John Jones as he comes in the library door, carrying a brief case.
      NARRATOR: "John Jones isn't here to borrow a book or research a business problem. Tonight he's fulfilling a community responsibility."
      CLOSE UP of door with sign "Library Board of Directors."
      MEDIUM SHOT of Jones passing through meeting room door.
      NARRATOR: "As an elected member of the XTOWN PUBLIC LIBRARY John Jones meets monthly with six other citizens of Xtown to ... (etc.)"
      REVERSE ANGLE of Jones sitting at the table, taking out papers from brief case.
      PAN SHOT of room, showing graphs, maps, posters, etc. of a busy library ....

8. How to edit:

a. Run all rolls of processed film, in the order in which they were shot, on your projector without stopping, just to gain an immediate reaction.

b. View the film several times more, taking notes on which scenes you can keep and which need to be re-shot and why.

c. Now, put on a pair of thin cotton gloves (so that you don't ruin film as you handle it) and run each roll through the 8mm editor machine. Cut out everything that is technically poor, irrelevant or redundant.

d. Tape together what you have. Look at it again. Cut once more, until you have a film that tells the story compellingly, or excitingly or dashingly or however you had intended the tone to be.

e. Tape once more. View once more and scrutinize with a keen eye for every detail that could distract or detract.

f. When you finally have the product time right and showing exactly what you had in mind, move to the next step of adding the audio part.

9. How to fit narration, sound effects and music to the film:

a. Go back to the original script. How well does it now fit with the visual element you have created? Change as need be. The visual image should take precedence over the audio in film making.

b. The audio can be added through a tape, as with a slide show or by having a magnetic sound strip put on the film while it is being developed or after the final reel is put together and thus recording the sound on the film directly. You will, however, need a <u>sound recording projector</u> in order to read the narration or dialogue into the microphone at precisely the right timing as the reel projects by.

c. Use the same "music up and down in volume" technique here as you would for tape recorders and add sound effects in the same way, too.

10. How to wrap it all up:

a. Take the whole reel, video and voice, to be reproduced for as many copies as you need.

b. When the original and copies come back, label each carefully. Keep the original with the script in a safe place for referral or further duplication if more copies are needed at some later date.

11. Presentation:

a. Always check out the room facilities and the equipment. Exercise care that you have extra bulbs, extension cords and a back-up film in case anything goes wrong.

b. Check the film after each viewing to make certain that it is in good condition.

12. Develop a budget:

a. Equipment: 8mm super movie camera (or 16mm if you want to go that way), tripod, two to four spotlights, 8mm editor machine, super 8 projector, screen, 8mm sound recording projector, zoom lens, long tape measure, film storage facilities, dark room for editing.

b. Accessories: film, thin cotton gloves, 400-foot reels, scissors, extension cords, projector bulbs.

c. Production costs: staff time, equipment upkeep, film developing and duplication of completed reels.

STEP 53: VIDEOTAPING and CLOSED CIRCUIT TELEVISION

If there is one element that combines flexibility with ease, it is videotape. Sight and sound go together just as easily for scripted material as they do for live situations. Thus, you can videotape a day at the library in five-minute segments or three-minute segments on the hour and come up with a fascinating montage, or you can videotape a story-telling session and play it back for new volunteers as a training session, or you can videotape a program by a prominent guest and play it back at a later date for those who missed the original. The possibilities are limitless.

The initial cost may be greater than the outlay for slide production, so you have to weigh the value such an option has against the constraints of budget. If you can operate any camera, you can operate a videotape camera. The requirements are less exacting than they are for movie making; however, one must recognize the capabilities of the medium and develop an instinct for focusing in on what is really pertinent. By analyzing TV programs you can learn from good camerapeople how to make the story interesting, how to use film making techniques to fullest advantage (shots of different duration and from varying angles) and how to determine the theme and advance it through the choice of what you film.

The advantage of closed-circuit television is that people at varying locations can enjoy a common experience without anyone having to be transported to a central meeting place. It is a boon for shut-ins, for communities in remote regions, for residents of large metropolitan areas where patrons can visit their branch libraries to share a common program with others all over the city, for linking people across a state or region to discuss issues pertinent to all.

This audiovisual capability is worth exploring. It's new, and it excites the imagination of patrons--"Come on down and be on television" is an invitation that brings out a lot of folks. If, when they come, they discover that the library has a lot more than tv to offer them, they might come back because it's worth their while.

PART XI: MEETING THE PUBLIC ON
THEIR OWN GROUNDS

INTRODUCTION

When legislators look for a place to cut expenditures, libraries are often at the top of that list. It's a fact of life. Why fight it?

"You say you're short of funds for books? Well, no need to allocate public monies. I've got hundreds of old books in my attic that I can donate and I bet almost everyone else in the state capital could do the same."

The town's mayor, a regular library user and long-time library booster, has no trouble convincing his council to allocate revenue sharing funds for library use.

"I don't know why your library gets all this statewide attention when ours works as hard as yours," said a board member from ATown. "Well, let's look at what's getting us the publicity," replied the BTown Library Board member. "It's not the figures on circulation or the number of card holders. It was our annual report as a document that most recently made the news." "Yeh," grumbled the man from Atown. "I saw that thing dolled up like a newspaper supplement. Seems like a waste of time to me."

"This is our fifth civic group coming to the library for a tour within the past month," wrote the librarian in her report. "The 'Reach Out and Tell Everyone' publicity program has really brought results. It is our first coordinated campaign. I do believe that the planning has made the difference."

STEP 54: GOVERNMENTAL BODIES.

1. State, National. Library associations have carried the responsibility of educating legislators on State and National levels, but greater success can be gained through one or a combination of the following activities by all local libraries:

    a. Join a professional library organization and support their efforts.

    b. Keep your State and National legislators informed:
        1) Keep an active file of elected and appointed officials from your (taxing) area. Data to include:

163

Date & Kind of Contact
Name of Official
Office Held
District
Addresses
   official
   home
Tel. No.
Committee Assignments
Special Interests
Library Voting Record

2) Place them on your library's mailing list for important reports. (The content and format (pulling power) of these reports will make the difference between them being read, remembered and saved or summarily thrown out.) Highlight pertinent sections of those reports for immediate attention of the recipient.

3) Write letters in regard to pending legislation: a) Refer to the bill by title and number (including initials of the house of origin); b) State your position as being for or against the bill and enumerate the reasons why; c) Summarize the impact as a result of passage or failure; d) Invite the elected official to contact you for further discussion; e) End on a positive, friendly note.

4) Keep a file of the special interests of any legislators who live within your service area (and therefore have a card from your library). As a matter of courtesy, since they obviously can't come in to browse, let them know when new materials of special interest to them are ready to circulate. If you give a full citation, they can obtain it wherever they are meeting, or they might drop by your library on a home visit.

2. Local, Regional

a. Maintain an active file of local (regional) governmental bodies. Data should include:
Date & Kind of Contact
Unit
Presiding Officer
Names & Office of Officials
Home Address
Tel. No.
Term of Office
Special Interests

b. A library representative--board or staff member--should be assigned to attend all meetings of each of the pertinent governmental bodies (one each to the corporate authority; to the school board; to the planning commission; to the transit authority; etc.) Keep track of this through a "Library Participation Survey" (see page 167)

1) Each representative should file a report to the library board and staff pointing out items of significance to the library (reve-

nue sharing; population changes; critical issues; financing; growth patterns; etc.) Make these reports <u>accurate</u>, <u>brief</u> and <u>clear</u>: a) Include a heading that tells to whom the report is directed; from whom the report is coming; what it is a report of; date of the report. b) Identify the meeting attended by name of the body; date, time, place of meeting; name of presiding officer. c) Number the items in your report consecutively (for easy referral). d) Maintain an orderly file of reports.

2) Each library representative to a governmental body should be on that body's mailing list* to receive: a) Notices of meetings and the agenda of upcoming meetings. READ the agenda before going to the meeting. Discuss items pertinent to the library with the Library Board president or the library director and establish the library's position. Ask to be placed on the roster to speak or to answer questions. (Items of concern might be a change in traffic patterns that makes the street on which the library is located one-way, or a housing development for the elderly, or a community centennial). b) Minutes of meetings. Check them for accuracy. c) All other data generated by that group, including newsletters, reports, etc.

3) Each representative to a governmental body should have training in how to be a representative. Formalize such a program through the Library Board: a) Know and practice the essentials of group dynamics, people-to-people interaction and parliamentary procedure. b) Recognize and practice the role of a library representative and speak in an official capacity for and from the library, setting forth only those philosophies and policies set by the Library Board. c) Be intimately informed about the library and the group to which you are an observer.

c. Keep your local (regional) elected and appointed officials informed about and alerted to the library:

1) Follow items 1.b.1)-4) under "State, National" (p. 163-164), with adaptations for your local situation. Elected officials should be made aware of strong local support for the library.

2) Send each body a copy of the library board minutes and invite them to attend library board meetings.

3) Maintain a "Library Data Center"**at points of gathering in local public governmental buildings to make it easy for employees, officials and visitors to be informed. Keep the brochures, flyers, posters, etc. current. Use attractive and sturdy racks.

---

*Establish the library as a local government "Clearing House" including notices and minutes of meetings, memberships, terms of office, election (appointment) schedule, purpose (By-Laws) of the group. Let people know that the library has this data.
**An attractive and sturdy rack with service brochures, booklists, bookmarks and other library data, with a sign that clearly states "LIBRARY INFORMATION."

4) Maintain a VIP (Very Important Patron) mailing list for all local (regional) officials and their families. Mailings should include notices, newsletters and booklists of new titles of special interest (just as you already do for many other patrons who enjoy mysteries, gothics, etc.)

d. Introduce candidates to the library before they are elected to office:
1) Have a special open house and tour for the library board and staff to meet all candidates as soon as the filing date is closed (and before the campaign begins to solidify positions). a) Prepare an informational packet for them to take home--include the annual report, a brochure of upcoming programs and a statement of how elected officials can benefit from regular library use. b) Give these candidates a chance to ask questions and to get to know the facility and the staff and board. c) Explain clearly what the library's relationship is to each body or office involved in the election. d) Determine each candidate's point of view toward the library so that you know where the library stands no matter who wins the election.
2) Follow up with a thank-you letter to each candidate and include an open invitation for each to use and support the library no matter what the outcome of the election.

STEP 55: GOVERNMENTAL AND NON-GOVERNMENTAL COMMUNITY SERVICE BOARDS, COMMISSIONS, ASSOCIATIONS, AGENCIES AND (CO-ORDINATING) COUNCILS (General or specializing in service to a particular age or population).

1. Maintain an updated file of all of these. Basic data to include:

NAME:

PRESIDING OFFICER: NAME
ADDRESS
TEL. NO.

MEETING SCHEDULE: DAY
MONTH
TIME
PLACE

KIND OF MEMBERSHIP:

CONDITIONS OF MEMBERSHIP (including dues):

BASIC PURPOSE:

PUBLICATIONS:

BY-LAWS ON FILE: ____YES ____ NO

LIBRARY PARTICIPATION SURVEY--YEAR _____
FOR GOVERNMENTAL BODIES

NAME OF BODY	PRESIDING OFFICER	ADDRESS	TEL.	MEETING SCHEDULE			LIBRARY REP.	REPORT FILED
				DATE	TIME	PLACE		

LIBRARY PARTICIPATION SURVEY--YEAR _____
FOR COMMUNITY GROUPS

GROUP	CONTACT PERSON	ADDRESS	TEL.	CHARACTERISTICS	STRENGTHS	NEEDS	LIBRY OUTREACH SERV. PROG. MAT.

MINUTES ON FILE: ____ YES ____ NO   YEARS: 19 ____ - ____

REPORTS ON FILE: ____ YES ____ NO   YEARS: 19 ____ - ____

LIBRARY TIE-INS:

2. Ask to be placed on their mailing list, especially newsletters and pro-grams of events for the coming year.

   a. Post these and keep them on file for reference.

   b. Watch for conflicts, duplications or opportunities to cooperate.

3. Maintain an active relationship with their PR officers, editors and pro-gram officers.

   a. Have the library included in their newsletters:
      1) Contribute a special column (regularly, occasionally)
      2) Note library materials, services, programs of special interest to their membership and to the people they serve.
      3) Publish a library calendar.

   b. Help them plan meetings <u>in</u> the library (tours, special programs put on by the library staff).

   c. Help them plan programs <u>with</u> the library to serve their particular constituencies or the public at large. Examples: 1) Jointly spon-sor a seminar for business people with the Association (Chamber) of Commerce. 2) Jointly sponsor a consumer workshop for people on a fixed income with the Retirees and Senior Citizens Council. 3) Jointly sponsor a "how-to" series on home repair with the Ur-ban Council. 4) Jointly sponsor a program for achieving certain badges with the Girl Scout Council.

   d. Maintain an updated, attractive LIBRARY DATA CENTER in each of the offices and centers.

4. Establish a system whereby library board or staff members serve on these bodies (on a rotating basis?) as part of their duties. In some cases, full, continuing membership may be essential (practical?), such as with Arts Councils.

5. Establish the library as a community partner with this sector. Keep in touch informally. Attend functions. Invite these community leaders to the library so that they become intimately aware of its capabilities as a service center and can advertise it right along with you.

6. Establish the library as a participant in all types of community events from the big yearly bash that's been part of that community since its founding to recently established festivals or promotional days. KEEP A CALENDAR OF COMMUNITY EVENTS AND DON'T GET LEFT OUT.

Assign a library staff or board member to be a general liaison for community events and have the library participate in a very visible manner.

STEP 56: HEALTH SERVICE INSTITUTIONS, CARING CENTERS, ALLIED AND PROFESSIONAL MEDICAL ASSOCIATIONS AND THEIR MEMBERSHIPS.

1. Maintain an active file of all health care facilities in your area:

NAME	ADD.	ADMISTR.	SPECIALIZATION	POP. SERVED	LIBRARY TIE-IN

2. Establish a working relationship:

   a. Arrange for a meeting at the library with all of these administrators; or, arrange to be present at one they organize to develop guidelines for:
   1) library outreach services and programs
   2) maintaining a materials collection for general use that is allied to health care
   3) placing pertinent library informational materials in each of the institutions, centers, offices, etc. (At nursing homes, stress large print materials, Talking Book Service, films; at obstetrical clinics or pediatric centers stress materials on family and child care, nutrition, how-to's on building furniture or decorating; in animal hospitals stress materials on pets; etc.
   4) contributing to their newsletters (Try some columns: "Examine Us," "Let's Talk about OUR Operation!," "9 out of 10 dentists prefer library books to prevent mind decay"
   5) advertising library outreach and inlibrary materials and services for the publics these institutions and professions serve
   6) encouraging referral to such programs as Talking Book Service and Homebound Service

3. Use the yellow pages of the telephone directory to build mailing lists of dentists, opticians and optometrists, physicians and surgeons, and veterinarians.

   a. Invite them to the library for a get-acquainted program just for them

   b. Build a RESOURCE LIST of people available for in-library programming (do this for the rest of the section, thus involving a broad spectrum of people)

STEP 57: EDUCATIONAL INSTITUTIONS, CHILD CARE CENTERS AND ALLIED PROFESSIONAL AND PARENTAL ORGANIZATIONS.

1. Maintain a basic file and keep it current:

INSTITUTION	ADMINSTRATOR	ADD.	TEL. #	POP. SERV.	LIB. TIE-IN

2. Work cooperatively with school librarians. Set up an informal and formal relationship as professionals.

3. Make contact with administrators:

   a. Set a special open house and program (or a series of them) to invite educators, parents and students to the library to become familiar with how home, school and library can work together for the benefit of all. (You will have to work out financial problems that come up when children who attend a consolidated school do not live within a tax-supported library area).

   b. Develop interlibrary cooperation procedures between the various schools and centers and the public library:
   1) Share resources.
   2) Work together to improve the literacy of all the people.
   3) Jointly sponsor programs, tutorials, workshops (creative reading, puppetry, crafts, leadership training ...)
   4) Regularly invite groups of children and their families to the public library for both special and on-going programs. Always send the children home with something tangible in their hands-- a bookmark, a poster, a project they have completed on their own.
   5) Develop a "BOOK BAG" program that places rotating collections of carefully selected materials in nursery and day care centers. Provide enough bookmarks so each child can have one to bring home as a reminder of hours and programs.
   6) Arrange for public library personnel to visit schools to talk up special programs.
   7) Plan together to avoid duplication of materials and efforts.

STEP 58: RELIGIOUS INSTITUTIONS; FINANCIAL INSTITUTIONS; PLACES OF BUSINESS AND MANUFACTURING; LABOR, CRAFT AND PROFESSIONAL ORGANIZATIONS, ETC.

1. Once again, build a file.

NAME OF GROUP	ADMINISTRATIVE OFFICER	ADD.	TEL. #	CONSTITUENCY	LIBRARY TIE-IN

2. Group, by group, over a period of time, invite people to the library

(e.g. Special Retail Business Night) or arrange to appear as a speaker at their meetings. Introduce them to what's in the library for them and ask for ways to better serve their needs--make it a working relationship.

3. Arrange for the library to be mentioned in their newsletters--announce programs, materials of particular interest to that group.

4. Place pertinent library advertising where their publics can see and use them.

5. Develop library outreach and jointly sponsored programs. There is a mutual kind of benefit to all--e.g. a business provides prize money for a poster design contest (see below) and gets a tax write-off and lots of free publicity; a professional organization (such as lawyers) provides a series of seminars at the library for the general public and gets a better public image; a bank stuffs library announcements in its monthly mailing and gets credit for public service....

STEP 59: THE ARTS.

1. Develop two lists. One for organizations and one for local people in the arts and advertising:

ORGAN.	ADMISTRATOR	ADD.	TEL.#	CONSTITUENCY	LIBRY TIE-IN

NAME	AREA OF SPECIALTY	ADD.	TEL.#	AFFILIATIONS	LIBRY TIE-IN

2. Establish formal working ties with the local Arts Council. Coordinate and share activities and expertise. Arrange for a library representative to sit on the Arts Council board as a member or as an ad hoc official.

3. Develop mutual advertisement and showcase programs.

4. Work cooperatively to create an arts calendar, to co-sponsor "culture buses," to provide artists-in-residence.

5. Work with separate arts groups for the benefit of both:

   a. Community Theatre
      1) Does a production need books as props or stage dressing? Give them discards in return for a program credit. Do the same for art work to hang.

2) Find out the season in advance and order playscripts, recordings and tapes and advertise that you have them--ask the Theatre board to help, too.

3) Schedule the theatre group(s) to set up displays and exhibits in the library in conjunction with a production. Place your own library materials out for patron borrowing on the spot.

4) Co-sponsor programs--how to audition for community theatre, the what and how of "backstage" work, the art of theatre make-up ...

5) Place a library display in the lobby of the theatre (maybe even check out materials to people who bring their library cards).

6) Initiate playreading or interpretative reading interest groups at the library. Invite a member of a theatre group for brief discussions on various facets of theatre (script analysis, casting, characterization, make-up and costuming; set design, lighting, management). As a culminating activity, go as a group to a live theatre performance.

7) Create a climate where local playrights can try out their scripts or actors can have a trial run for auditions.

8) Co-operatively organize a traveling troupe to bring live theatre to people who can't or ordinarily wouldn't have the opportunity (schools, shelter care centers, malls ...)

9) Start a library collection of all theatre programs. Just think what that will mean in 100 years!

b. Artists, artisans, craftspeople
1) Provide a permanent display area for sale, rent and exhibit of works of local (area) residents. (Be certain the insurance needs have been covered). Highlight an artist a month or whatever....

2) Purchase original pieces of art for the library's permanent collection. Provide data about the artist and the medium.

3) Set up displays of pertinent books at gallery exhibits. Co-sponsor opening receptions--provide library informational data as "take homes."

4) Work with local artists, etc. to provide lectures, demonstrations, classes in the library or co-sponsor programs in galleries and arts centers. Provide for everyone--art as rehabilitation, etc.

5) With arts groups, co-sponsor an annual library poster and book-mark design contest. Co-operate with local business and industry to provide worthwhile cash prizes and a promise to print and distribute the winning design.

c. Musicians, dancers and groups of ...; retail outlets for music, instruments, recordings
1) Bring live music to the library both as a part of receptions and as mini-concerts. Give the audience a chance to meet with and talk to the performers.

2) Lend music--in its many forms--as part of the library's regular service. Safeguard sheet music by making a double seal of clear adhesive paper.

3) Co-sponsor "choose an instrument day" or "what's my style of

singing week." Bring in teachers to share their expertise.

4) Develop a mutual trade-off with shop-keepers. They advertise the library in their shops, the library sponsors programs where they come in and talk about "how to buy stereo equipment" or "what to look for in a band instrument" or "how to choose a dance or voice teacher" ...

5) Have professional entertainers plug libraries during their acts at local clubs. Keep these people on your list of priority mailings to let them know when materials of special interest to them are ready for circulation.

6) Develop a special section of local recording artists and advertise your wares when these people are appearing, whether it is locally or on TV.

d. Writers, editors, publishers and the advertising council

1) Develop a special section in the library for the published works of local writers--collect memorabilia and ephemeral materials (working drafts of manuscripts, newspaper clippings, taped interviews, etc.) Regularly feature a local writer and his/her works.

2) Co-sponsor autographing parties with local bookstores. Turn it into a media event.

3) Co-sponsor readings--poetry, works-in-progress, dramatic interpretations.

4) Work with editors and publishers to provide programs to share their experiences and expertise--"How does advertising sell?"; "What's the difference between an editor and a publisher?"; "What's a columnist?"

STEP 60: SERVICE AND SOCIAL CLUBS, FRATERNAL AND INTEREST GROUPS.

1. Maintain an updated file of all of these groups. Use the format from Step 55 and the LIBRARY PARTICIPATION SURVEY on page 167.

2. Establish a library staff member as a good program for their meetings. (see APPENDIX A: Giving a Speech Is a Way of Communicating)

3. Invite each group to visit the library as a program. Issue library cards on the spot.

4. Build a basic library volunteer program from this group (see PART XIII).

5. Send library data to the program chairperson so each member has constant information about what's new and what's coming up.

6. Feature a local group each month--invite each to put up a display that tells about what and how the group contributes to the community.

7. Invite them to place the library on their public service list and to provide funds for special projects that they work out with the library director (a service group can supply that new sign for the library or new shelves or a yearly subscription to a magazine in large print.)

8. Invite them to sponsor special interest groups in the library, such as a chess club, or conversational French, or aquaplaning, etc.

9. Invite them to give a series of programs--a demonstration of the martial arts, a demonstration of glass painting, etc.

10. Provide a worthwhile service to organizations by having the library put together a series on "Club Organization". Topics can include: How to run a meeting; How to write by-laws and amend them; How to publicize; How to write minutes; How to set up successful fund-raising projects. At these sessions, display and circulate library materials to supplement the topics.

STEP 61: REACHING PEOPLE WHO DON'T BELONG TO ANY ORGANIZATIONS.

By systematically working through what you consider to be every layer of community organization you may assume you have received everyone in your service area. In reality, there are some people who don't come under any heading. These people should be library users, too. Thus, you will also want to place information about the library in places where people gather.

1. Search the yellow pages of your telephone directory. Make a mental note of the categories of retail businesses.

   a. If yours is a community with one main shopping area, take a fresh look at these stores during a walking tour. Make a note of which places have a good-looking front window display that would enhance some library materials.

   b. If yours is a somewhat larger or very much larger community with several shopping areas, work with a map and pinpoint where there are clusters.

   c. Do the same for recreational areas (movie houses, bowling alleys, roller skating rinks) and service shops (hair salons, auto repair, tv/radio/stereo repair).

   d. Either you or a staff or volunteer member working on "Information Outreach" should inspect these areas for tie-in possibilities.

2. Once you have targeted opportune locations:

   a. Contact the manager or proprietor.

b. Describe the library's interest in reaching as many people as possible and how a tie-in with that place of business would help.

c. Offer library materials for window displays along with the store product or service, with a nicely lettered sign that goes along with their theme, as well as materials for in-store display in areas that will catch interest.

d. Ask if handouts at the cash register would be appropriate.

e. Establish this contact as a library user and convey enthusiasm for the proprietor or manager and all other store employees to want to "talk the library up."

3. Release feature stories to mass media about these cooperative efforts. (You might attract some volunteers).

4. Here are some ideas:

a. RETAIL STORES
    1) Front window displays. Working with the store display designers.
        a) In fashion shops have mannequins holding best sellers, classics, records, magazines, etc. from the library with a sign: "YOU'RE ALWAYS IN FASHION AT THE LIBRARY. WHY NOT DROP BY TODAY?" On an additional sign give the library hours and location. Back to school time is a good tie-in for retail stores and libraries. b) In department or drug stores compliment the make-up department with book jackets on cosmetics and skin care. Book jackets on successful letter writing can be placed at the stationery counter. A window display can invite people to follow the yarn line to "Learn how to be a better consumer" or "How to use this product to better advantage," etc. Let people know these materials are at the library. c) In furniture shops, have library books on the center table along with a sign that says: "Every lovely piece of furniture is enhanced by a conversation piece from the Xtown Library." Place library materials on end tables, bookshelves, night stands, furniture for children and infants, etc. Identify them as library materials and place appropriate book lists with library location and hours alongside the book jackets. d) In grocery stores, have books on nutrition, cookbooks and home entertaining right along with the canned, packaged and fresh products. Create special interest centers with spinach and Popeye; dog food and Snoopy; cookies and Sesame Street's Cookie Monster
    2) In-store displays. Working with department personnel, use books and store merchandise (with appropriate backdrops). a) Show crafts items made from patterns and designs from library books and materials from that shop. b) Illustrate how a book on photography influenced work done by a local amateur photographer. (Because crafts and photography shops sell books, use the idea: "NOT CERTAIN WHICH BOOK TO BUY? BORROW SEVERAL

FROM THE LIBRARY, COMPARE AND PURCHASE THE ONE THAT SUITS YOU BEST".) c) Specialty shops offer all sorts of opportunities--re-enact a scene from a murder mystery using their wares; set up an expedition and put out all your books on exotic places; create a sequence ranging from big picture books to story books in a toddler's and young person's shop, with appropriate clothing articles arranged.

b. FAIRS, MALLS
1) Be an exhibitor--co-sponsor a booth or area with other libraries or another agency or group in your community.
2) Co-sponsor an entertainment or a prize.
3) Arrange for media coverage of such activities.

c. IN MOVIE HOUSES, BOWLING ALLEYS, DISCOS, BARS, ROLLER SKATING RINKS, ETC.
1) In the movie house lobby, along with popcorn, display book jackets of books that have been made into films. At specific times set up a 'browsing' display and issue library cards and circulate materials.
2) In discos, put up "flashy" posters that announce that musical recordings and "how-to-dance" recordings are available at the library.
3) In bars or clubs fold foldover advertisements of the library on tables. Make them attractive to entice users to the library. Emphasize materials that are right for the clientele of each place--from gothics to Chilton manuals.

d. IN SERVICE SHOPS
1) Along with the in-shop supply of glamour magazines and Hollywood exposés, place several well-aimed flyers and brochures of library materials and programs in hair salons, figure improvement centers, and laundromats.
2) In auto repair shops hand-outs and posters on consumer data and travel seem appropriate.

e. AT SPORTING/SPORTS EVENTS

1) Negotiate with the ticket office to enclose a library flyer with tickets. Gear the contents of the flyer to pertinent materials (tennis bibliography for a tennis event, etc.)
2) Place a multi-faceted display panel in the lobby area of the arena (etc). Attract attention with give-away balloons.

f. IN PARADES
1) Join them! Suit yourself up as a foot-parader or dress up the bookmobile or enter a float or festoon a flotilla of cars.
2) Give away inexpensive carry-bags with the library imprint.
3) Have fun, make friends and keep the library visible.

g. IN TRAIN, BUS STATIONS; AIRPORTS

Hang posters of high visibility

5. This listing gives you a few basic ideas. Individualize for your community, but get out to "bring 'em in." Work at it systematically. Don't try to cover everyone at the same time. Blitz tactics are nice for the moment but what do you do for a follow-up? Develop a five-year plan, otherwise choose a time sequence that's right for your area.

DATE	TARGET GROUP	PLAN OF ACTION	EVALUATION

6. A very special type of "INFORMATION OUTREACH" is one that compares library registrants with people listed in the city directory (or telephone book). A note can be sent to those people who don't have cards. (Example: "We notice that you don't have a library card. Since you are a taxpayer you are entitled to one. Enclosed is a coupon to exchange for your card. Come in any (days) during (hours). We'll be happy to give you a tour of your library.") Follow through by sending the same coupon and an appropriate message to newcomers through the Welcome Wagon.

7. The basic thrust of all of these efforts is to have the library be a vital, functioning, necessary part of the community. When people think of the top five services, the library should be one of them.

STEP 62: PUBLIC OPINION RESEARCH.

Find out what people think of the library and why. Devise your own surveys, invite a college class to use your library as a practice study or hire a firm to do it, but be honest in your approach, careful in your tabulations and forthright in your follow-up. Basically, people like to know they are being consulted.

1. Define your reasons for carrying out public opinion research.

2. Develop an instrument that will fulfill the objectives stated above.

3. Be prepared to publish the results and to follow up on the findings.

4. Choose one or a combination of the following kinds of public opinion research tools:

    a. Image surveys: These determine what people think of the library, how well its services and materials are known, and what people like or dislike about the library.

    b. Motivation Research: This finds out why people use or don't use the library.

c. Effectiveness Surveys: These are used to find out how effective library publicity and advertising and public relations really are. Often, it is used as a 'before and after' technique--finding out first, how much the public knows about the library and what the general attitude is and then, after a planned informational campaign, asking the same questions and comparing the results.

d. Content Analysis: This deals strictly with finding out how the library is treated by the news media. If you want to find out on what pages library stories appear, what kinds of headlines are used, how often and in what light the library is covered, etc. by a newspaper, you set up a model by which to make these judgments. Essentially, you did a content analysis when you prepared for work in PART IX.

e. Individual Public Studies: Rather than going to the public as a whole, you may want the views only of one particular sector--say, People in Education or People in the Retail Trade.

f. "The Public Relations Audit": Before starting off on a publicity campaign you may want to know what is the best way to get your library message across to each audience. This means carefully analyzing the responses to the public opinion tools listed above in the light of your own views of the library. Thus, you may ask yourself (and your staff and board) to answer the same questions as you asked of certain publics and then compare the two kinds of responses. You thus become very aware of how your own perceptions may color what and how you advertise. You can try this with a simple device: have people at random complete this sentence: "To me, the library is _____." Compare the responses of users to those of the library personnel. The point here is to help you advertise in a way that will appeal to the public you want to reach, not to advertise in a way that you think will appeal to that public.

g. How to use public relations research:
    1) To correct misconceptions--When you find out what a group thinks it knows about the library, and that is an erroneous conception, it is your job to correct that error in thinking.
    2) To give you information about peoples' needs--If you don't intend to do anything about what you learn, don't research in the first place. If, however, you do intend to act, you may discover that you need to give some new kinds of services or get rid of some you've been trying to give away with no takers.
    3) To develop favorable attitudes--As you learn more about your publics and how they view and use the library, you can provide even better service for the users and at the same time help everyone gain more respect for an institution that is too often taken for granted.
    4) To let people know that the library really cares about them as individuals, not as mere groups or statistics on the annual

report--You may ask, "Can you find what you need in this library? ____" and follow that with, "What changes would you make?" When people see you making the changes they suggested, they'll feel a lot more kindly disposed. And remember to acknowledge both privately and publicly this kind of responsible feedback.

5. Soliciting Suggestions

a. The traditional SUGGESTION BOX with paper and pencil handy. Place several boxes around the library, and perhaps in other locations in the community.

b. Set up a tape recorder into which people can speak their suggestions.

c. Nearby either of the locations of the box or the recorder, or in a newspaper article, or in a brochure, post or tell people what action the library has taken on each suggestion.

d. A DILEMMA BOX. If the library is facing a problem, present it to the public and ask them how they would like it solved. Give a choice of solutions from which to choose or leave it wide open. Inform the public on the outcome.

e. HOW DO YOU ... slips of paper in library materials that are checked out. If you want to know about a specific service, ask directly through a two- or three-question communication. Tabulate the results and report:
    HOW DO YOU like the new library hours?
                    or
    HOW DO YOU prefer to work in the library:
                    ____ at tables seating several people
                    ____ in private carrels
                    ____ on soft chairs
                    ____ on the floor on a rug
                    ____ (other) _____

STEP 63: THE BOOK TRADE.

Librarians deal with books as the mainstay of their collection. How much do you know about books, besides that they have to come and go in your library to make it worth your while to be there?

1. Book publishers:
    a. Why do they publish what they do?
    b. How do they decide on publication schedules?
    c. What goes into determining the cost of each book? If you don't know the answers to these questions, invite a publisher in to provide a program just for your staff and board and to talk shop.
    d. Communicate with publishers. Tell them if the format of the books

they are putting out is poor. Tell them that you need a stock of standard titles to replace the worn out volumes people keep borrowing. Tell them what patrons are telling you.

    e. Are you listening to publishers through their publications, at book exhibits and fairs and at professional conferences?

2. Book sellers:

    a. Do you have a systematic way of buying books or do you buy from whoever comes along with a trunkload that you can get inexpensively (so you think)?

    b. Can you get what your patrons want fairly quickly or do you have to keep them off with an exasperated, "It's been on order for two months. It seems to take forever to get the books." And yet that book is on sale at the local book store and has been for the past two months.

    c. Do you have a recourse or do you have to put up with a jobbers' delivery schedule?

3. Retail book trade:

    a. How well do you know the stock of book retailers in your area?

    b. How do you work together to promote reading?

    c. How often do retail book merchants come to the library?

4. Inventory your answers and come up with a plan of action to help you meet this very important library public on their own grounds, along with all the others.

PART XII: PROGRAMMING

INTRODUCTION

At the height of "Tutamania" Xtown library featured a local resident's slides and narrative of his trips to Egypt and his research into the Nile Kingdoms.   There was standing room only.

Each of the series of eight different crafts demonstrations-workshops attracts about 25 people, with half as constant comers.   This means that many new patrons enjoy a library service of their particular interest.   In three years the range of topics has been from batik to weaving.

In a two-months' period the library featured a local expert on China in a five-part discussion series; needlepoint classes; local high school art works on display; creative dramatics for the younger children; an exhibit of arrowheads collected by a patron; and a senior-citizen review of books for children.   The population of the community is around 1000.

STEP 64:   AN OVERVIEW.

1.   Establish where you want to provide programs sponsored by the library-- in the library or outside of the library.   Write objectives in terms that are obtainable through specific activities.

2.   Conduct (annually) a community profile to:
   a.   Determine existing audiences and their specific interests (go back to the wealth of data you have from PART XI)
   b.   Determine what is already being done by other local groups and agencies--avoid repetition and competition
   c.   Determine how you can tie the library in with other groups and agencies to make the library impact stronger--share resources, budget, publicity

3.   Locate resource people, using a variety of resources including:
   a.   Patrons with specific talents to share in your setting
   b.   Subjects of newspaper feature articles with talents to share
   c.   Residents of neighboring communities who have provided good programs in those libraries
   d.   People from PART XI (and the Yellow Pages of the telephone directory under specific businesses, organizations, etc.)
   e.   Personnel in schools, universities and governmental agencies with

specific expertise

    f. Artisans (find them at arts and crafts fairs)

    g. Special interest groups that sponsor special days, weeks or months of wide interest

4. Interview each individual to be certain that each is dynamic, informed and alert to audience (or individual) reaction--in short, you want a good program source.

5. Create and constantly update a PROGRAMMING RESOURCE FILE:

Name	Talent/Topic
Address	Tel. No.
Availability	Program specifics

Cross-reference under topic and name.

6. Build a programming idea file based on:

    a. Annual inventory of community interests, or

    b. Survey by the Citizen's Advisory on Library Programming, or

    c. Patron requests (set up a programming idea box that is visible)

7. Develop a yearly calendar of programs. Include:

    a. Continuing programs for all ages and interests (Story time, Home bound ...)

    b. Annual programs (Summer, "Spook Day," "Pet Day" ...)

    c. Special programs (Exhibit of New Zealand artifacts, How to Curb Maple Tree Disease ...)

8. Follow through on program development:

    a. Check community calendar so as not to duplicate topics

    b. Establish goals that can be reached

    c. Get the personnel to plan, carry out, conduct, follow through on the programs for the year

    d. Set details for each program (See PROGRAM PLANNING, pp. 191-194.)

9. Build money for program development into your library budget:

    a. Foreseeable expenses--staff time, room use, equipment, materials, publicity, transportation, refreshments, custodial, thank-you's and gratuities or gifts, staff development

    b. Contingency fund

10. Publicize the package and the individual program:

    a. Zero-in on the specific target audiences for each program--unless being general is to your advantage.

    b. Use all of the publicity resources available (integrate a book-list in all advertisement flyers).

11. Evaluate the year's programming and each individual program:

    a. Did the program achieve its purpose--why, why not?
    b. Did you meet a community need?
    c. What changes should be made, how, by whom?

12. Follow-through:

    a. Be certain each person who helped is thanked.
    b. Review the guest book for each program and keep in touch with each patron through other mailings for materials and other services.
    c. Return all borrowed materials.
    d. Inspect all equipment so that it is always in good repair and ready for use.
    e. Always have alternative plans in case a program falls through and something else must be substituted at the last minute.
    f. Always have alternate accommodations in case a conflict or problem arises.

STEP 65: PROGRAMMING ALTERNATIVES.

1. Programming with People

    a. The Lecture
        1) One speaker who is an expert on a particular subject giving a preplanned speech.
        2) A person who introduces the speaker, is alert to needs during the speech and coordinates the Question/Answer session at the end before thanking the speaker and the audience for coming.
        3) A person who coordinates the program by: a) Contacting the speaker and communicating precisely what the topic is; the level and age of audience; the length the talk is to be, the rules for the Question/Answer session and any follow-through. b) Getting data for the introduction and publicity. c) Seeing to it that the physical needs are met: adequate seating space, lighting, ventilation; amplification system; lectern; water for the speaker; any A-V equipment to specifications.
        4) A lecture can fulfill any of 3 purposes: a) present information to a group of people by an "expert." b) stimulate a group to act by a "believer." c) analyze or criticize by a critic.
        5) Audience can participate by asking questions of the speaker

    b. The Dialogue
        1) Two articulate people speak extemporaneously from a common experience through a sharing of ideas in a give and take process on an agreed-upon list of points.
        2) A program co-ordinator arranges the program, introduces the

participants and the topic and steps out of the program until it
it is time to close with a succinct statement to wrap it all up.

3) Mostly used to inform in an informal, conversational setting.

4) Audience can participate by asking questions of the participants
either during the discussion (if that is agreed upon) or following
the set time limit for the dialogue

c. The Panel

1) Consists of at least two articulate, informed people with different
views on a particular subject and a moderator who poses specific questions relevant to the topic for each panelist to speak to.

2) Several views on a subject are presented so that audience members are challenged to think and to formulate and articulate their
own ideas.

3) Panelists can present a formal statement and interact with each
other.

4) Discussion can: a) Be from the floor with the group as a
whole interacting within a specific framework over which the
moderator presides. b) Be in small discussion groups with a
skilled discussion leader for each. c) In either case, recorders document who says what.

5) A concluding statement drawing together the ideas of the group
is presented at the conclusion by the moderator.

d. The Symposium

1) Consists of at least two articulate, informed people who present
different aspects on a particular topic and a chairperson who
introduces each speaker and topic and who at the end weaves it
all together.

2) The co-ordinator must be sure each speaker knows the full
scope of the program so as to avoid repetition or blank spots.
A planning meeting with all participants often avoids problems.

3) Used to inform a group (can cover a controversial topic but the
presentations are geared to be informative rather than provoca-
tive).

e. Role Play

1) Used in the discussion of a problem where people need to understand each other's point of view.

2) A skilled leader establishes the problem and the objectives before setting the guidelines for the "acting out" of roles.

3) Player-participants are each "given a role"--the opposite of what
is their true-life situation--and, without rehearsal, are asked
to defend their "role" position.

4) The leader breaks off the role play at the right point so the
group--all participants--can discuss and come to a concensus
about resolving the problem.

5) Sufficient space for moving around is essential, and the group
may best be in an informal horseshoe setting for the discussion.

f. Discussion Groups

    1) A group gets together, sets its objectives and the manner in which it can reach them, selects a leader and goes about carrying out its program based on the specific points that need to be covered.

    2) Informality is the key--the leader must create immediate rapport with the group, keep it from straying from the subject and summarize.

    3) An informal arrangement of furniture for seating is important.

    4) A recorder captures the essence of the discussion.

    5) There is a common concern or interest among a group that is more-or-less equally informed on the topic.

    6) Acquiring depth of understanding of the topic is usually more important than reaching a concensus.

g. The Demonstration

    1) Used to show manual operation ("how-to-do-it") or interaction between people ("how to act") so people gain confidence to go out on their own.

    2) Requires a person or persons who know the subject well enough to show it meaningfully to a group.

    3) Take-away materials are often essential for follow-through.

    4) Adequate space and materials with which to work need to be provided.

    5) Can be linked with a lecture ("Show and Tell") and can incorporate A-V materials along with the actual objects.

h. The Workshop

    1) Used to give people a chance to learn how to do something or to gain greater skill in something they already know how to do.

    2) Requires a leader who can demonstrate and then guide people "to do it" successfully themselves.

    3) Preparation of sufficient materials and adequate work space are essential, along with "take home" instructions and samples.

    4) Advertise the materials participants are to bring.

i. The Orientation to Use the Library

    1) Used to give people specific skills and confidence in using special or all aspects of the library, its various departments, services and range of materials.

    2) Conducted by a person knowledgeable and capable of transmitting, within a positive framework, skills and confidence to the particular group.

    3) An opportunity to learn by doing and materials for reinforcement to take away are essential.

j. The Library Tour (See TOUR PLAN, pp. 188-189).

    1) There are three options: a) Spur of the moment. b) Planned as a regular service (specific hours for people to sign-up for). c) Planned as a special service (group activity reserves a specific time other than that for regular tours).

2) Requires careful planning: a) Where to meet group. b) How to greet group. c) Sequence of the tour--tailor for the size and interests of the group. d) Length of time--allow for rests and questions. e) How to end tour (refreshments, packet of data to take home).

k. Entertainment
1) People come together as an audience to enjoy a performance.
2) A printed program of the sequence and an explanation are provided at the event for the audience to follow.
3) An opportunity to meet the performers in an informal setting, with light refreshments, is a bonus.
4) A coordinator makes all arrangements, including providing ushers to seat the audience and all special effects for the performers.

2. Programming with Audio-Visual Materials

a. Films (8mm, super 8, 16mm, 35mm; silent, sound; feature, cartoon)
1) Co-ordinate with a booklet or run by itself.
2) Program around a theme or generalize.
3) Tie-in with any of the preceding options or as a culminating activity to view in one sitting scenes from a year-long series.

b. Slides
1) A slide narrative program that is live or taped can also fit in as a lecture program or as a workshop for learning "how to" create a slide show.
2) Automatic change and sound equipment can provide an individualized programming device useful in malls, at fairs or exhibits.

c. Filmstrips
1) Used with aspects of the previous programming options under "People ..." or as a self-sustaining individualized program option
2) A fun workshop program for young people to create their own filmstrips.

d. Video-tapes
1) The participants become "stars" on TV
2) View home-made or "canned" materials as a program

e. Exhibits (discussed in PART VII)

3. Programming with Telephones

a. Dial-a-Story, etc.

b. Telephone Reference Service

c. Telephone Tape Center

(cont. on p. 190)

TOUR PLAN

DATE	STARTING LOCATION	STARTING TIME	ENDING TIME	ENDING LOCATION	NAME OF GROUP	CONTACT PERSON	TEL. #	ADDRESS	INTERESTS

TOUR PLAN (cont.)

TOUR PLAN SEQUENCE	WHO WILL GREET	WHO WILL GUIDE	MATERIALS	REFRESHMENTS	EVALUATION OF TOUR

    d.   TTY for the deaf

    e.   Phone-a-book (Book waiting at Circulation desk for patron to pick up)

Develop these after careful consultation with the Telephone Company that services your area and basic research of models, their successes and failures.

4. Programming with Automation

    a.   Computer learning centers for individualized work on specific topics.

    b.   On-line search capabilities for individual patrons.

5. Programming with Books

    a.   Book Fairs

    b.   Pre-packaged book packs (call or stop by at library to order for specific dates)
        1) For the ill child or adult--picked up by a friend or relative and contents based on interests of the recipient
        2) For visiting relatives
        3) For a trip
        4) For day care centers
        5) For nursing homes

    c.   Regular mail-box delivery and return for shut-ins

    d.   Paper-back trade-off at:
        1) Terminals and stations
        2) Court House
        3) Medical clinics/hospitals
        4) In the Library

6. Programming for Visibility

    a.   Sponsor a sports team or event (little league or bowling team; annual library tennis or golf or ... tournament)

    b.   Sponsor an annual event in conjunction with a holiday or a community event (Frog jumping contest, horseshoe throw, poster contest)

    c.   A room in the library can serve as the "local office" for state and national officials

    d.   A desk at the library can be an advance ticket distribution center for sporting or musical or theatre or ... events scheduled in the community

e. A desk at the library serve as a voter registration and voting machine demonstration center

7. Programming for Specific Needs

a. Develop an on-going "language for travelers" tutorial program

b. Duplicate 'home-made' cassette tapes as a patron service

c. Give special attention to:
   1) Expectant mothers (work directly with physicians to build the library habit)
   2) Newly weds (send a note of congratulations) invite both to get library cards (or one, as need may be) and include special materials like "Setting up a spice rack from scratch," etc.
   3) Children entering first grade
   4) New teachers to the schools in the community
   5) Newly named executives
   6) New city employees
   7) New residents (Welcome Wagon)

d. Schedule regular meetings with school personnel (Media Specialists, principals), Parks and Recreation Director of the community, Senior Citizen Center Director, Arts Council Director, etc. to coordinate

8. Programming for Outreach (See PART XI)

a. Bookmobiles

b. Mini-centers for materials

c. Information Centers for data about the library

d. Talks to community groups

STEP 66:   PROGRAMMING PLANNING AIDES.

THE SUMMER LIBRARY PROGRAM FOR YOUNG PATRONS

1. Clearly stated objectives:

Theme:

2. Guidelines:

a. Starting date: Ending date:

b. Age range:

c. No. books:

d. Kinds of books:

e. Reporting plan:

f. Staff needs:

3. Budget:

ITEM	COST
Record keeping	
Certificates	
Awards	
Displays	
Posters	
Flyers	
Bookmarks	
Refreshments	

4. Materials Preparation

PRODUCTION SCHEDULE	PERSON IN CHARGE	LOCATION OF PROD.

5. Publicity Plan:

VISITS TO SCHOOLS	LOCATIONS	DATES	CONTACTS

MASS MEDIA RELEASES

6. Activity Plan:

Sign up date: time: place:

Reporting dates: times: place:

Special events:

7. Evaluation:

Participants
Resource people
Library staff
Parents

8. Follow through:

Thank you notes:
Re-cap to mass media:

Return of borrowed items:
Ideas for next year:

9. Where to get ideas:

    a. Take-off on current topics of interest to children.

    b. Buy a complete program.

    c. Borrow from other libraries.

BASIC PROGRAM PLAN

NAME OF PROGRAM _____

COORDINATOR   AREAS OF RESPONSIBILITY   DEADLINES

ASSISTANTS

BUDGET:

INCOME SOURCE   AMOUNT   EXPENSES ITEMS   AMOUNT

DATE(S) _____

TIME(S) _____

PLACE(S) _____

AUDIENCE _____

REGISTRATION

    DEADLINE: _____ TO: _____
                                  (name)   (address)
    COST: _____ PAYABLE TO: _____

OBJECTIVES:

RESOURCE PERSONS: ADDRESS   TEL. #

PROGRAM STRUCTURE
      ACTIVITY   TIME   LOCATION   PERSON IN CHARGE COST

PHYSICAL NEEDS   WHERE GET   WHERE RETURN   COST

MATERIAL NEEDS   WHERE GET   WHERE RETURN   COST

FLOOR PLAN

PUBLICITY PLAN (Use materials from PARTS VIII + IX)

MEDIUM   DEADLINE   PERSON IN CHARGE   COST

PHYSICAL CONTINGENCIES:

ALTERNATIVE PROGRAM:

EVALUATION:

    WERE THE OBJECTIVES MET?   WHY?   WHY NOT?
    DID THE PLAN WORK?
    AUDIENCE REACTION?
    SUGGESTIONS:

FOLLOW-UP:

    THANK YOU NOTES:
    MASS MEDIA WRAP-UP:

PART XIII: DEVELOPING A BASE OF COMMUNITY RESOURCES FOR ONGOING SUPPORT

INTRODUCTION

Public spiritedness is one of Xtown's greatest assets. Residents are justifiably proud of their beautiful library and we of the staff try to do our part by going that "extra mile" in service.

Summertime and it's hot. What to do? Turn the residents on with a lemonade day. The following year we did it again. Five years later, we added a pet show to keep Lemonade Day exciting and we got three weeks of continuous coverage in the local newspaper and record turnouts of people.

We have seen our Friends change its emphasis over the dozen years it has been in existence. We started as an informal group to campaign for a new library building. We enjoyed ourselves so much we decided to incorporate as a non-profit organization to raise funds to furnish the new building. Now we find ourselves training as volunteers to give another kind of service.

The most important thing to acknowledge is that you can't do it alone. The library has to be people-oriented in serving and being served. When I reached out into the community and said, "I need your support to make this a better library for you," I became a good librarian.

STEP 67: ORGANIZING SUPPORT THROUGH ACTIVITIES.

1. <u>To Advertise</u>
   a. On a rotating, monthly basis, each of the businesses and industries that mails to the entire community adds a library mailer to its envelope so that the library incurs no postage expense. Develop a chart to help you get each item to the right place on the date needed:

DELIVERY DATE	DEL. LOC.	DEL. CONTACT	COMPANY	PR ITEM	STAFF MEM. IN CHARGE

b. On a rotating, monthly basis, each business that advertises in the area newspapers runs, in their ads, a tag-line about the library's programs for that month. Develop a chart to help you get the data to the right place on the date needed:

DATA DEAD-LINE	CONTACT PERSON & ADDRESS	BUSINESS	MESSAGE CONTENT	STAFF MEM. IN CHARGE	FOLLOW UP

c. Annually, specific businesses salute the library during special weeks, including Children's Book Week and National Library Week. Designate the contacts you need to make and the approach you will take. Work with their advertising personnel to get the message right.

d. A group of businesses sponsor a weekly five-minute "LIBRARY UPDATE" program on the local radio station(s). Make preliminary contact with the business association to determine feasibility.

e. Annually, a civic group underwrites the cost of having quality library materials distributed through the Welcome Wagon program.

f. Annually, a civic group provides a corps of people who "SPEAK UP FOR THE LIBRARY" and who provide entertaining and informative programs before other groups. Assist the "corps" in developing their program and monitor their activities throughout the year. Give appropriate recognition.

2. To Assist

a. A Friends of the Library group is organized with specific aims to assist the library.

b. Library Volunteers are organized and trained to carry out specific functions that enable the library to better serve the various needs of a broad base of the community.

c. A civic club assumes the responsibility of providing a specific service.

d. Fund raising activities are co-ordinated by a core group that is experienced in developing a tradition of giving, be it through used book sales, deferred giving, bequests, living memorials, matching grants. This group can raise funds through entertainment, sales of services and benefits.

e. Specific civic groups develop and maintain collections through the donation of a sum of money, and through expertise on the subject. (Lions establish and maintain the Large Print collection; Rotary, the International Children's Books Collection; Mental Health Association, the mental health shelf; etc.)

    f.   Advisory Boards, Councils or Committees are organized with specific representation that covers every phase of community economic, political and social strata. These groups work with the library administration to set priorities of services and materials and to provide the support base for programming.

3.   To Lobby

    a.   A Library Support Group or a Task Force on Libraries or a Coalition of Citizens, made up of people representing already established groups (such as Association of Commerce and Industry or Chamber of Commerce, labor unions, Affiliated Clubs, school boards, Ministerial Association, League of Women Voters, Newcomers, Retired Persons, etc.) act as a clearing house for legislative action on libraries. They garner support for legislation when needed and express appreciation to those elected officials who vote for the necessary library funding.

    b.   Library board members become active political advocates of the library.

4.   To Co-sponsor With

    a.   Organized groups (resource list available as a result of your activities in PART XI: MEETING THE PUBLIC ON THEIR OWN GROUNDS) and the library work co-operatively.

    b.   Ad hoc groups organize for the purpose of providing special programming or a one-time event or a special recognition (anniversary, centennial, autographing party for a local author, current events, etc.)

5.   Steps Toward Action

    a.   List those activities the library is now involved with that would go better if you had support.

    b.   List those activities you would like the library to be involved with but aren't because of lack of funds, staff or expertise.

    c.   Next to the items on both lists jot down the names of groups and individuals who can be approached to fill in the gaps.

    d.   Bring these lists to your board and ask for support staff to get a program ("LIBRARY ASSIST") going and maintained.

STEP 68:   ORGANIZING SUPPORT THROUGH EXISTING GROUPS.

When groups already exist, you may need to re-evaluate with them whether their present functions are those that are most crucial to the library or whether their extremely loose structure makes them "invisible."

1.   Friends of the Library

   a.   Did they organize to pass a bond referendum, and with that accomplished they continue to meet once a year and to run an annual used book sale? Could the group become actively involved in other ways?
      1)   Ongoing: a) Organize a group of Friends as "Tour Guides" for classes, groups and regular tours. b) Provide weekly service to the homebound and people in nursing homes. c) Provide craft classes for young people and adults. d) Maintain the local history collection.   e) Co-ordinate a program of community displays and exhibits in the library.
      2)   Special: a) Conduct a community survey to determine what residents get from the library, what they would like to get, what they need. b) Publish a community directory of organizations.   c) Publish a community directory of free and inexpensive programs for groups.

   b.   Do the Friends shy away from the political scene? Suggest that they organize another branch that is involved only with being a legislative watchdog.

   c.   Do the Friends prefer fund-raising through bake sales? Suggest that they organize another group to go after the big money grants and donations.   (Work with the people in the community who have expertise in money raising techniques.)

   d.   Are the Friends shy about advertising that the library accepts large bequests and memorials of all amounts? Suggest that they sponsor a Task Force whose sole purpose is to solicit these kinds of funds for the library.

2.   Volunteers

   a.   Did they organize to provide programs for children, but now the library has a staff member for this function? Could the inactive group serve in other ways?
      1)   Outside of the library: a) Programs for people in nursing homes. b) Programs for Peace Meal centers.
      2)   Inside the library: a) Work along with a library staff member to halve the time in which some technical aspects are completed. b) Carry out some of the research aspects of community service for which there is no staff time provided (see PART XI).

3.   Maintaining Library Support Groups

a. Are you able to maintain interest in the two library support groups mentioned above? If not, why not? Are they recognized as groups and individuals? Do you have a system of recognizing three-year members, five-year, etc.; officers; outstanding achievement; etc.? Do you recognize volunteers for specific hours of work? Do they receive certificates, pins, flowers on their special days, a reception in their honor during Volunteer Recognition Week? Are you generous with news releases about the work these people do? Do you ask for their input or always tell them what to do? Do you evaluate and plan together? Do you constantly attract new people to keep the groups vital with fresh enthusiasm and revived spirit? Do you encourage people to move into new areas as their confidence grows? Are you able to get a project started, make sure it is operating efficiently and then move away from it, with the understanding that a Friend or Volunteer is now responsible for it and that you are available in emergencies?

b. New Friends and Volunteers need a good orientation to the library, its goals and capabilities and how their effort fits into the total picture. They need a handbook as a reference tool and continuing education to be updated and to keep informed.

4. Family of Staff and Board

Are these the "great overlooked" resource? Can they become a tremendous positive PR resource? Sponsor a tea for these people--including spouses, children, aunts, uncles, cousins and all sorts of kin. Find out what they think of the library. Level with them that they can be the best spokespersons or the worst enemies. Find out what the library is doing wrong if the general attitude towards it is negative. Solicit their help in putting things right so that they can go out and "sell" the library. Meet informally two or three times a year to talk over common concerns and to share in-put. Appoint each family member as a deputy PR officer and give each the appropriate name tags and calling cards. Feature them in the library newsletter. Run a "Spotlight on our Boosters" feature weekly (or monthly) with a photo of a family member (name included) on a library bulletin board.

5. Separate Groups That Support the Library

In any given community, any number of organizations or businesses give money or in some way provide services or programs to the library. They have no link with each other, except for a common interest in the library. If one member from each of these groups sits on a special board that is an umbrella for these diverse groups, and if all of these people together project an image of "clout" in a political sense, the library commands a greater degree of visibility than it does when this widespread support is not organized. Such a group need meet only once or twice a year, to be toasted by the library board and staff in appreciation for the financial and personal support they give, and to review the quality of the support each offers (do needs change?). They can be given a name of significance to your community as a distinguishing factor. The name should reflect their importance and should serve to attract others to want to be a part of it. It is this kind of support that helps the library establish itself as a vital, responsive community service, whose budget must never be jeopardized.

STEP 69: ORGANIZING NEW GROUPS.

1. General outline for organizing a Friends of the Library*

   a. Either a library board member or someone from the library staff should be designated to study the advantages and disadvantages of creating and maintaining a Friends group for that community. A deadline for a report to the Staff and Board should be set.

   b. If the report is positive toward a Friends group and the Board authorizes the formation of one, a coordinating committee is appointed by the Library Board president. The committee should be made up of Board, staff and community members, with an appointed chairperson.

   c. The tasks of the committee should be spelled out and a time line should be established. It should be clearly understood that all action by the coordinating committee is subject to Library Board approval.
   Tasks can include:
   1) Drafting by-laws. The by-laws should include:
      Article I.   Name of the Organization.
      Article II.   Objectives (purpose)
      Article III.   Membership
      Article IV.   Board of Directors and Officers
      Article V.   Duties of Officers
      Article VI.   Election of Officers and Term of Officers
      Article VII.   Standing Committees and their duties
      Article VIII.   Meetings: General and Board of Directors
      Article IX.   Amendments
      Article X.   Dissolution contingency
      Article XI.   Order of business
   2) Incorporating as a non-profit organization under the laws of the state and in accordance with the dictates of the Internal Revenue Service.
   3) Planning a program of activities for the first year.
   4) Designing a membership recruitment campaign (Charter Members).
   5) Organizing the initial meeting at which officers are elected and

---

*Based on data from various libraries and from open discussion at the "Friends of the Library Workshop" sponsored by the ILA Public Library Section on Sept. 26, 1979, in Decatur, Illinois. See also Robert's Rules of Order Revised, pp. 284-291, for steps in establishing an organization.

standing committees are appointed.
6) Presenting a final report to the Library Board and dissolving.

d. An effective publicity campaign* should spell out specific answers to logical questions:
1) How did the need for a Friends group arise?
2) Who is a Friend of the Library?
3) What do Friends do?
4) Why be a Friend?
5) When and where will the organizing meeting be held?
6) With whom do Friends work?
7) What does the library now offer?
8) What difference in services, materials and programs can a Friends group make?
9) Will there be any fun in being a Friend?

2. General outline for organizing a Library Volunteers program

a. Library Board appoints a committee to study the feasibility of organizing a volunteer corps, and sets a deadline for the report to the Board.

b. If the report is positive toward a Volunteer Corps and the Board authorizes the formation of one, a committee is appointed by the Library Board President. The committee should be representative of the various departments of the library, a cross-section of the community from which volunteers will be recruited, a Board member and at least one person experienced in working with and organizing volunteers.

c. The tasks of the committee should be itemized, a time line should be set and it should be clearly understood that all action by the committee is subject to Library Board approval. Tasks can include:
1) Defining precisely what each volunteer is to do
2) Writing job descriptions
3) Establishing supervisors and a line of communication between staff, volunteers, Board
4) Writing a handbook or manual for volunteers
5) Organizing an orientation and continuing education program for volunteers
6) Establishing how volunteers will be recruited, placed, trained and recognized for service freely given
7) Preparing the staff for integrating volunteers into the library routine

d. An effective publicity and recruitment campaign should be organized and carried out.

---

*Based in part on a handout created for The Vespasian Warner Public Library, Clinton, Illinois; Malinda Evans, Librarian.

e.   The program should be initiated, with the proper degree of publicity at the outset and a plan to re-new interest with a publicity campaign on three-month cycles.

f.   The committee should continue to function in an advisory capacity, with membership changing as the need arises, under the jurisdiction of the library board.

3.   <u>Coordinate the development of community resources, on a yearly basis, with a monthly itinerary:</u>

COMMUNITY RESOURCE BASE ORGANIZATIONAL CHART

(month)   (year)

<u>DAY   DATE   ACTIVITY   GROUP   CONTACT PERSON   ADD.   TEL.</u>

4.   <u>Monitor all support activities to insure positive PR</u>

a.   The relationship between staff, board and support groups must be an open, friendly, sharing one. If any friction begins the source must be immediately tracked down and removed.

b.   A happy friend will spread a thousand glad tidings. A disgruntled friend will cast doubts where none before existed. Keep all support groups happy.

c.   Before initiating any support group provide for the following:
1)   Good orientation to what that particular contribution is all about in line with the entire operation of the library
2)   A chance to meet informally with all of the human elements that make up the library
3)   A handbook that can easily be updated
4)   Interviews with library staff who will be directly involved or affected
5)   Continuation of information through workshops, programs, mailings (that fit into the handbook, perhaps of three-ring binder type)
6)   Recognition within the community and beyond its corporate limits
7)   Programs for retention, growth and continuous recruitment to replace natural attrition (people move away, become ill, change jobs)
8)   Periodic evaluation so as to keep on top of needs that are changing and needs that are emerging

PART XIV: THE LIBRARY BOARD AND PR*

STEP 70:   ACTIVITIES TO INITIATE AND CARRY OUT PR.

It is no longer a question of why bother with PR.   Library Boards now recognize that without an ability to respond to user needs and to interpret their library to each individual patron and to each governmental entity their library will lose its financial stability.   In an age of fiscal accountability the LIBRARY BOARD is the agency solely responsible for showing who benefits how for the dollars that are spent.

1. The library board sets the tone and establishes proprities regarding PR as:
    a. A board function
    b. A staff function
    c. A community support function
    d. A professional function
    e. A political and economic function **

2. What does the library board member need to know to make valid PR decisions?

    a. Why the library exists as an information agency in that community
    b. What individual and group needs the library presently meets
    c. What individual and group needs the library presently does not meet
    d. What resources are required to close the gap between present performance and fulfillment of what each individual has a right to expect and receive from the library
    e. What the components of a good library PR program are †

3. How can the library board design the PR program?

    a. Appoint a Task Force (using the resources from Part XI) on Library Relations to Its Publics composed of representatives from local:

---

*An excellent base of reference is the MISSION STATEMENT FOR PUBLIC LIBRARIES prepared by Public Library Association of American Library Association in conjunction with the White House Conference on Libraries and Information Services.
**See "Funding of Public Libraries: Some Dollar Stretching Techniques", Illinois Library Association, 425 North Michigan Ave., Chicago, Ill. 60611.
† See "The Trustee and Public Relations" by Virginia H. Matthews, pp. 121-129. THE LIBRARY TRUSTEE. 1978, Bowker. ed. Virginia G. Young.

1) Business and Industry
2) Labor, Professional and Vocational groups
3) Civic and Cultural groups
4) School and other Educational Institutions
5) News Media and people in the Public Relations professions
6) Governmental Bodies and Elected Officials
7) Cross-section of Users (balancing age, economic levels and social strata)
8) Cross-section of Non-users (balancing age, economic levels and social strata)
9) Health Service and Recreational institutions
10) Religious institutions and Minority groups
11) Cultural agencies and institutions
12) Organized library support groups
13) Library staff
14) Library board
15) Library Public Relations Officer (specialist, consultant, or whatever the title is)

<u>OR</u>

Appoint a permanent Board and Staff Committee on Library Public Relations

b. Charge the Task Force or the Committee to:
1) Survey the community to: a) Determine community and individual information needs. b) Evaluate library performance. c) Analyze the degree of awareness on the part of residents regarding the library's potential as a source of information and recreation. d) Analyze the library board's and staff's awareness of how the public views the library.
2) Design a five-year public relations program to reach every segment of the community so everyone living there now and everyone moving in is continuously aware of "what is in the library for them, personally" and so that the library has periodic feedback.
3) Recommend a budget (including personnel, equipment, materials, etc.) to accomplish each goal.
4) Provide an annual progress audit and, with the staff and board as a whole, chart the next year's course.

4. How can library board members actively participate in an ongoing PR program?

a. Because the public looks to the library board as being their representatives and as having the ultimate power and responsibility for the operation of the library, the board must be in control. Thus, the primary task of any library board member (elected or appointed) is to maintain a clear and open channel of communication with all levels of governmental structure. The Board, as an entity, must be visible to (other) elected officials. The board must participate in local government budget discussions. The board as a whole must speak up so that other governmental agencies respect the right of the people to have full and open access to information through the library. A CLOSE AND CONSTANT ASSOCIATION WITH (OTHER) ELECTED OFFICIALS leads the list of PR activities.

b. Because the library staff looks to the library board to set the standards of service, the board members must be aware of how well their library compares with minimum standards as established by the ALA. As the fiscal agent, the board is charged with getting the most for the least cost. But, as trustees of an institution that has been at the cornerstone of democracy, the board is challenged to provide the best services, materials and programs that money can buy. RESPONSE TO USER NEED, TRANSLATED THROUGH THE STAFF, is the second PR responsibility.

c. Because community leaders look to the library board members as the spokespersons of the library, the members will need to be articulate about the operation of the library to the general public and to the mass media. Board members must be available to appear before any group for a program, to sit on commissions involved with community growth, to establish the library as a worthy recipient of tax deductible grants, bequests and matching funds. Board members must also be aware of what the mass media is reporting or editorializing about the library and must respond accordingly, either to express appreciation or to correct. ACCEPTANCE OF LEADERSHIP WITHIN THE COMMUNITY is a third PR expectation.

d. Because library users look to their library board as a channel of communication with other agencies, board members must be alert to cooperative possibilities that will strengthen all units. KNOWING WHAT IS GOING ON IN THE LIBRARY WORLD, AND IN ALL OTHER POSSIBLE WORLDS, is a fourth PR challenge.

e. Because non-users (erroneously or not) look to the library board as an "elitist" group, library board members must correct the error and engage in special projects that provide a better understanding of what the library, as a community agency, can offer to people who aren't book or information oriented. BUILDING BRIDGES, NOT BARRICADES, is the fifth PR ingredient.

f. Because the library profession looks to the library board to provide the broad base of collective support through participation in library associations, the library board member must look beyond the immediate local situation. INVOLVEMENT WITH LIKE-MINDED INDIVIDUALS WHO CAN SHARE EXPERIENCES AND FRUSTRATIONS AND LEARN FROM EACH OTHER is a sixth aspect of PR.

5. How can the library board expect to carry off PR responsibilities along with its fiscal and policy making mandates?

a. A committee structure provides a framework. Working through the strengths of each individual trustee (library director), the board president can name chairpersons from the board and appoint two or three members from the community-at-large and/or staff to work with each board member in a specific area. (With every segment of the community involved, in one way or another, with the library, there's a lot of continuous constructive support and awareness building going on--the most importatn goal of PR).

b. A staff member should be given the authority to co-ordinate the PR support program, as articulated by the board, along with the daily advertising of library materials, services and programs.

c. A careful and effective library board orientation enables each board member to assume leadership roles within a short time after taking a seat on the board. Having worked with the library board through a committee or task force responsibility prior to election or appointment to the library board further strengthens that individual's capability for instantaneous contribution.

6. How can the library board translate its PR philosophy to the staff and public?

    a. Review the rules
      1) Are they restrictive, antiquated, subject to misinterpretation?
      2) Are they "yes" or "no" oriented?
      3) Are they positive, upbeat and valid from the patron's point of view?
      4) Is there room 'at the discretion of the staff member' for error? It may be necessary for a task force to re-write the rules.
      5) There are rules but no one knows where they are, if they are in print or how they came to be.
      6) The rules change with the librarian on duty.
      7) Everyone sort of understands the rules--that is, until new people move in. It may be necessary to re-evaluate the procedure so that some uniformity exists. It's hard to have effective PR if people are unhappy. RULES EXIST FOR THE BENEFIT OF ALL.

    b. Review the staff handbook
      1) Does it convey an attitude of cheerfulness and competency?
      2) Are job descriptions clear and performance reviews fair?
      3) Are benefits in keeping with economic and social conditions?
      4) Are orientation and continuing education sessions built into the job?
      5) Is there a definite program of recruitment, retention and recognition of staff? Being a good employer and creating a happy working environment are essential to good public relations. A staff that is recognized is one that will perform well. (See **PART XV: PR ASPECTS OF STAFF MANAGEMENT**)

c. Keep library board meetings open
   1) Invite staff members to regularly report to the board and to provide programs for the continuing education of library board members.
   2) Announce library board meetings for anyone to attend, but make it a habit to regularly invite specific patrons to visit and comment.

d. Sponsor recognition days
   1) With the library director plan periodic programs for recognition of staff, volunteers, friends, committee members and patrons. Set the rules--length of service, outstanding service, department of the month or whatever, but be fair and be consistent until everyone gets a chance.
   2) When someone retires or resigns make it a happy going-away with a recognition ceremony.
   3) Celebrate birthdays, anniversaries of programs, the 1000th caller in the newly installed books by telephone program, etc.

e. Recognize the service of peers
   1) Board members should show the public that they are a team that cares about each other. Thus, retiring members should be recognized, special service should be recognized.
   2) Leadership in trustee organizations should be encouraged as a community contribution.

f. Periodically attend library staff meetings and community library advisory meetings.

g. Expect to receive and to react to reports filed with the library board by staff and citizen participants in library-oriented programs and community groups (See PART XI).

7. How can the library board promote its library and staff within the profession?

   a. Library board members individually and the library as an institution join library organizations and regional interlibrary cooperation efforts.

   b. Budget items be included for travel to and participation in meetings, seminars, workshops. Board and staff members develop their specific expertise into a workshop format for presentation on an interlibrary cooperation basis and at conferences.

   c. Subscriptions to professional journals provide for a wide base of "keeping up with the field." Smaller communities can co-ordinate and share subscriptions. A set routing sends each issue to everyone on schedule.

(Cont. on p. 211)

ACTION PLAN OF CITIZENS FOR AN IMPROVED LIBRARY OF _____

POSITION	NAME	ADDRESS	HOME TEL.	WORK TEL.	DEADLINES	TASK DONE
REFERENDUM COORDINATOR						
CONSULTANTS						
Legal						
Financial						
RESEARCH COORDINATOR						
Legal Election Procedure & Election Authority Liaison						
Analysis of local elections						
Alternative campaign procedures						
Campaign budget*						
Tax exempt status						
CAMPAIGN FUNDRAISING COORDINATOR						
Donors $100 +						
Donors $99-$25						
Donors $24-$ 1						
CAMPAIGN STRATEGY COORD.						
Campaign Design						
Campaign Calendar						
Campaign theme and advertising plan						

* Be careful to adhere to local and state laws.

POSITION	NAME	ADDRESS	HOME TEL.	WORK TEL.	DEADLINES	TASK DONE
Support groups:						
Recruitment						
Assignment & Training						
Voter lists						
Registration of voters						
Voter Contact:						
Telephone						
Door-to-door canvass						
Letters						
General Meetings						
Neighborhood meetings						
Special groups						
Election Day:						
Poll watchers						
Telephoners						
Transportation						
Baby sitters						
Count watchers						
Emergency						
PUBLIC INFORMATION COORD.						
Legal Notices						
Speakers' Bureau						
Media						
Ink Print Advertising						
Display Advertising						
Target groups						
"Truth Squad" to counter opposition						
FOLLOW-UP COORDINATOR						
"Thank you letters"						
Evaluation & Report						

ACTION PLAN (cont.)

POSITION	NAME	ADDRESS	HOME TEL.	WORK TEL.	DEADLINES	TASK DONE
Scrapbook & Publications						
Legal Filing*						

*Be careful to adhere to local and state laws.

d. Board and staff members allow time in their schedules to share successes, results of research and ideas through publications. By studying the contents of professional journals, expertise is gained as to where to send each item. Basic contributions to major journals include:
1) a clear, glossy, black and white photo of an event, a program, a display or an exhibit, with an accompanying brief caption.
2) a brief narrative description of the above,
3) articles of varying length that are based on research or offer a philosophy or challenge readers to action.

e. Beware of solicitations for contributions of ideas, sample handouts, etc. "for a future publication." These solicitors take what hundreds of well-meaning librarians send them, publish the material under their name and make lots of money selling the book back to those who submitted the material for free!

8. How can the library board provide for the public's acceptance of change and growth for the library?

a. A library board that keeps in touch with its constituency will have the support it needs when capital improvements or a building program become necessary. Good communication and careful planning are at the bottom of any decision for a referendum. See pages 208, 209, 210 for an outline for an action plan to get organized and monitor each step.

b. Library board members who run an efficient operation will be alert to changes that require large outlays of money and will prepare the public for such eventualities. The reasons and the advantages will be documented and available.

c. A public aware that the board bases its decisions on careful evaluation of research and consultation with a broad base of users will respond in a positive manner to changes in policy and procedure.

d. A good board perpetuates itself by attracting qualified people to accept positions when vacancies occur. Stability and infusion of new ideas combine to make the library board a vital organization.

PART XV: PR ASPECTS OF STAFF MANAGEMENT

INTRODUCTION

In the past month, two people offered positions in YTown Library turned down the jobs. Why? By word of mouth they had heard that it's a miserable place to work.

Grilled, interrogated and badgered at the interview, clerical applicants never want to see the place again.

Returning to the library where she had been a student clerk years before, the woman found it to be as delightful a situation as she had remembered. She gladly recommended it as a good place to work to a young graduate student.

The interviewee accepted the position. The interviewer was delighted. They had had such a pleasant conversation, neither had gotten around to discussing the specifics of the job. The shock came on Monday.

Mr. Z is known for completing every compliment with a put down: "That's an OK sign, but I would have done it this way...." "That was a nice program, but too many people were there. I've never seen half of them before...." "That was a really good article. Several people commented on it. But don't you think it was a little long?"

"Everytime I look in the want ads I see there's an opening at our library. Isn't it wasteful to spend all that time hiring and training new people continuously?"

"I'll say this for our library director. We don't miss him when he's gone."

A nomination for "boss of the year" read in part: "Our library director puts the support staff on a professional level. He provides opportunities for meeting with clerical people from other libraries. He encourages continuing education that includes visits to office supply centers to see first hand what's new in office technology. He makes 'the back room' the first tour stop and says that it's here that service with a smile starts. We never know on whose desk a flower or a note will magically appear. He kids us about a secret admirer but we know the source. We've learned from his example that caring about each other and working as a team advances us individually more quickly than does competing...."

212

The staff is the most visible human element in the library. People get a mind-set about a place based on the atmosphere, which is communicated through the decor of the physical facilities and the attitude of the staff. Thus, it is essential not only to have a place look good, but also to have that institution's staff project a brightness, cheerfulness and competency that says, "I like what I'm doing and I'm particularly pleased to be doing it with you."

STEP 71: STAFF SELF-INVENTORY FOR "SMILE LEVEL".

At a staff meeting, or whenever the staff gets together casually, each should list the things that:

1. S/he likes (or enjoys) about your library.

2. Make her/him happy about her/his work.

3. S/he would also like to do at the library.

4. S/he has especially noticed about the community.

5. S/he has been able to participate in as a resident of the community.

6. S/he thinks people in the community think about the library.

7. S/he knows about recent action and/or the general philosophy of the Library Board.

8. S/he knows about the work of library support groups and who is involved.

9. S/he likes about the public relations plan of the library.

10. S/he thinks is her/his special contribution at the library and to the community.

STEP 72: ANALYZE THE INVENTORY.

The staff should then get together to talk over their responses. Strengths and areas where communication needs to be improved will become apparent. Brainstorming and open discussion should develop a plan that will help put a genuine smile on everyone's face.

STEP 73: THE 3 R's (RECRUITMENT, RETENTION, RECOGNITION).

If good communication is at the bottom of every happy situation, how do you place on the following?

YES   NO

____ ____   a. We have a terrific staff. We aren't afraid to tell it to each other.

____ ____   b. There are booster posters in the staff room. We all contribute.
> "This Is a Sign of Success"
> "People Are What We Most Care About"
> "We Deliver More Than We Advertise"
> "A Smile Is Worth 1000 Words"

____ ____   c. There is a means for staff members to express their feelings without repercussion. We have a BUGGED BOX and printed notes that invite blowing off:
___ bugged me at work today.

____ ____   d. We use "yes" often, both for the staff and patrons.

____ ____   e. We say "thank you" to each other even when patrons are listening.

____ ____   f. We save our "patron gripes" for the staff room.

____ ____   g. Discuss problems quietly and look for solutions together.

____ ____   h. If a staff member does something wrong, she/he deserves to be chewed out right then and there.

____ ____   i. Interviewees for positions get a tour, meet the staff and are designated a "friend" of the library even if they don't join the staff.

           j. The staff handbook contains the following items:
____ ____   History of the library
____ ____   Community profile
____ ____   Philosophy of service
____ ____   Profile of current library people (board, staff, support groups, committees)
____ ____   Scope of the collection
____ ____   Community resources as backup
____ ____   Floor plan of the library
____ ____   Personnel code (job descriptions, performance review procedure, benefits)

____ ____   k. The entire staff has access to Library Board reports and time to discuss them.

____ ____   l. The staff meetings have a set agenda and always include a short informative program.

YES   NO

____ ____ m.   Each job description allocates time for reading, sharing and discussing professional literature.

____ ____ n.   Continuing education is built into the personnel code as is time for reporting on attendance at workshops, seminars and classes and on books of value.

____ ____ o.   Staff orientation and training follow a specific format.   An "old" employee is assigned to a "new" employee on a "buddy system."

            p.   Information sharing procedures within the library are right for its size:
____ ____   word-of-mouth
____ ____   signed memos
____ ____   bulletin boards
____ ____   newsletters on a regular basis
____ ____   staff meetings
____ ____   written reports

____ ____ q.   Nice notes periodically appear in pay envelopes: "Thank you for the extra work on displays this month" "Your suggestion put into practice has improved the check-out service.   Keep those ideas coming."

____ ____ r.   There is a formal recognition for 5-, 10- (etc.)-year employees.

____ ____ s.   The staff lounge is a bright, pleasant, energizing stimulating place.

____ ____ t.   There is a planned termination interview for all employees, no matter what the circumstances for departure are.

____ ____ u.   Staff training includes sensitivity towards what makes patrons happy.

____ ____ v.   Employee incentives are written into the job description.

____ ____ w.   Social events are part of the working conditions without interfering with service.   This includes recognizing birthdays, special honors, holidays, etc.

____ ____ x.   Participation in community service is encouraged and rewarded.

____ ____ y.   Time is allocated for membership in and participation with professional associations.

YES   NO

____   ____   z.   Everyone has a comfortable and adequate area for work.

STEP 74:   ASSESS THE 3 R's IN YOUR LIBRARY.

1.   Make a list of the plus items:

RECRUITMENT   RETENTION   RECOGNITION

2.   Make a list of improvements needed.   Give them a priority rating:

RECRUITMENT   RETENTION   RECOGNITION

3.   Decide how to institute the improvements.

APPENDIX A: GIVING A SPEECH IS A
WAY OF COMMUNICATING*

Librarians are uniquely qualified to provide programs for civic groups, business meetings, academic gatherings or any place that people gather to listen to someone else. Librarians are especially suited for talking about libraries outside of the library. But, many librarians lack the skills to put their expertise into words. For those who are "unaccustomed ... to public speaking ... " we offer an easy invitation to learn how simple the operation really is.

To COMMUNICATE EFFECTIVELY you must be concerned with: 1) what you want to say, 2) the order in which to present your ideas, and 3) the manner in which you deliver them.

First, decide exactly what it is you want to say. The content depends upon the audience and the time limitation given to you:

a)   Did the program chairperson give you a specific topic?
"What's new at the Library"
"Books for the vacation-bound"
"Programs for children and young adults at the Library"

b)   Is there a special program or service you want to plug?
"Classes in creative stitchery"
"Non-print materials"
"Books for business men and women"

c)   Do you need to introduce the full range of library services to a group of newcomers?
"Your library has something for everybody"

d)   Do you need to solicit support for funding, or a positive vote in an upcoming referendum election, or participation in a Friends group or in a library sponsored community project?

e)   Do you need to inform the community-as-a-whole about significant changes at the library?

*By Rita Kohn, for a Corn Belt Library System Workshop, Normal, IL, September 15, 1976. Published in Library PR News, November/December 1979 (vol. 2, nos. 11 & 12), pp. 13-15. Reprinted by permission.

"We've moved and you're welcome to visit our new home"
"The renovation is completed--come look us over"
"We can offer even better service with our new circulation system"

Second, determine what effect you want your speech to have:

a) Do you want more people to come to the library to use its services and materials?

b) Do you want more people to spread the word about specific services and materials?

c) Do you want more people to support expanded services and materials?

d) Do you want more people to volunteer services or to donate money and materials?

After you have determined your TOPIC and PURPOSE, OUTLINE your speech. Each speech has three parts: a beginning (introduction), a middle (body), and an end (conclusion).

The INTRODUCTION must accomplish two things: 1) interest the audience (catch each listener's attention), and 2) state the speaker's purpose. Commonly used attention-getting devices include:

a) Establishing common ground with the audience, that is, saying something you know they will be familiar with.

b) Telling a joke or anecdote relevant to the topic.

c) Using a quotation that captures the central point of your talk.

d) Asking a pertinent question, the answer to which is your central point.

The CENTRAL IDEA of your presentation must be presented in a single sentence that is clear to both you and your audience. You should also make clear what approach you will use: report, explain or argue.

a) A weak statement reads: "I'm going to say something about the library."

b) An effective statement reads: "Centerville Public Library has services and materials for all residents of this community. Today I'll introduce five specific areas and invite you to visit the Library at 525 North Shady Street to see the full range of what is available. Hours are listed on the brochure you'll receive at the close of the program."

The BODY must elaborate on the specific points you are making and bring your audience around to the action you intended. The length depends upon the time allotment.

The CONCLUSION should restate the central point and show why and how the audience can act on the points you have made. There must be a connecting link between the introduction and the conclusion. When the speech is done, the audience should recognize that what was said is relevant to them and they should be clear about their line of action. For example, "These five areas are an example of the range of services available to children, young adults, adults, the elderly, businesspeople, farmers, students and professionals. We, of course, have much more available for all residents of Centerville, and the library staff looks forward to having all of you stop by the Library to browse, chat and borrow. And remember to ask if you don't see something you need."

Knowing what you want to say and the order in which you are saying it is two-thirds of the communication plan. The other third is concerned with three basic points: 1) sentence structure and word choice, 2) coherence, and 3) delivery.

Sentences should be short and clear. You can vary the structure, but take care that a listening audience does not lose the point. Choose words that have universal meanings and that say what you mean. Verbs, adverbs, and adjectives can provide color and excitement. Define technical terms. And, by all means, use supportive illustrations and materials to make your points clearly. You can bring along a display showing what is available and provide handouts for people to take home as a reinforcement of what you are telling them. You may issue library cards on the spot, check out library materials right then and there, sign people up for a committee assignment. In this way, when you say that libraries are an action place, you are illustrating on-the-spot your choice of a word!

Your speech must hang together. Be sensitive to the situation of the audience. Valid guidebook points of advice include: don't introduce extraneous materials; don't go off on tangents; don't bring in a story that has nothing to do with the point of your speech; don't talk down to or above your audience. To help your audience stay with you as you develop your points, state that you are making five points and then clearly specify: 1,...2,...3,...4,...5,...

Be sure your pronouns have clear antecedents--to whom does "he" refer? Use transitional words and phrases--"however," "specifically," "to illustrate what I mean".... Reiterate your central point every so often, and show how your examples support that point.

Give your audience time to digest what you are saying. Provide time for questions and interaction from the audience. Provide writing tools if you want the audience to take notes.

Delivery is contingent upon the audience. Who are they? How much do they know about the topic? What is their attention span? How interested are they in the topic? How large is the group?

Delivery also depends upon your best style. Do you read a speech well? Do you work better from notes? Do you know your subject well enough to speak "off-the-cuff"?

Volume and speed are important factors. Be loud enough to be heard and slow enough to be understood. Watch for audience reaction. If they are straining, looking bored, fidgeting, take inventory of your delivery immediately and make the necessary adjustments.

Be natural, comfortable and friendly while speaking. Use those gestures that are part of you. Avoid choppy hand movements, taking off and putting on of glasses, twisting of top buttons, fidgeting with your watch, shuffling papers.

And, above all, have eye contact with your audience--all of it. Try to give the impression that you are talking <u>with</u> each person, individually. If you are reading the manuscript, know it well enough to be able to lift up your head every few seconds without getting lost or flustered.

Thus, to communicate effectively through a speech, know exactly what you want to say, build your speech so it has a clear beginning, a supportive middle and a conclusive ending. Be concerned with audience appeal through short sentences, clear words, ideas that hang together and careful delivery.

Librarians have nothing to lose and much to gain by making themselves available for community programs. The timid can learn, the bold can polish speechmaking techniques.

APPENDIX B: WRITING A BOOK FEATURE*

A book feature may be written to entice readers to the library, to advertise books, to spotlight a topic/subject or to critique/review books. The <u>purpose</u> of the book feature will determine the technique and books you will use in the feature.

BASIC TIPS

1. Find out the newspaper column requirements:
    a) how long should your article be
    b) how should the article be submitted:
        margins
        pica or elite type
        double spacing
        paragraphing
    c) deadlines
    d) editorial do's and don'ts

2. Establish who in the library has responsibility for overseeing the column: establish with whom you will work on the newspaper staff

3. Set a schedule:
    a) a weekly column, a monthly column ...
    b) one contributor writing all of the columns,
        contributors on rotation,
        guest contributors with a library coordinator
    c) specific topics on specific dates throughout the year

4. Design a column title and logo that expresses the image of the library and provides a good identification for the newspaper reader.

5. Identify in what section of the paper the feature will regularly appear.

6. Allow for adequate writing and research time in your work schedule.

7. Decide on a writing style that is compatible with your community.

---

*Prepared for a Resource Manual for a Demonstration/Workshop "You Can Do It" by Krysta Tepper and Rita Kohn at the Corn Belt Library System, Normal, Ill. on February 14, 1979.

8. Decide on the top number of books you'll discuss in any one column.

9. Evaluate your column by keeping track of how many people ask for the books you "wrote about" or how many generally comment on the piece "they read."

BASIC ALTERNATIVES

1. An ANNOTATED LISTING on a particular topic/subject or a potpourri that provides title, author and a three-or-four-sentence summary (without either telling the whole plot or gushing about how exciting, thrilling, worthwhile or important this and the other nine books are).

2. A FAMILIAR ESSAY that works its way into mentioning titles, authors and content as part of the point of the "written conversation."

3. A FORMAL ESSAY that addresses a topic/subject of current interest and that has as its objective the discussion of books that fall under that heading.

4. A CRITICAL/COMPARATIVE ANALYSIS of the works of a particular author or of a particular subject or genre or of one book by itself.

5. A COLLECTION OF SHORT COMMENTS by preview readers who have been asked to provide their opinions for just such a purpose.

BASIC STEPS TOWARD PERFECTING SKILLS OF BOOK FEATURE WRITING

1. Read what other people write about books and analyze their content and style in relation to your needs. Good sources are professional journals and publications such as JUNIOR PLOTS and INTRODUCING BOOKS.

2. Decide exactly why you are writing a particular column, what point you want to make, what reaction you want to get. Then choose the materials and the format of the column.

3. Dig in and write on your own. You will gain confidence as you go along. Follow logic by constructing your written piece to satisfy a reader and not leave him/her wondering what you are saying--or why. Try your column out on someone who will be honest and fair with you before sending it in.

4. Re-write only if the article needs it, not just because you feel insecure.

BIBLIOGRAPHY

BOOKS & PAMPHLETS

Angoff, Allan, ed. Public Relations for Librarians: Essays in Communications Techniques. Westport, Conn.: Greenwood Press, 1973.

Blumenthal, Lassor. The Complete Book of Personal Letter-Writing and Modern Correspondence. Garden City, N.Y.: Doubleday & Co., Inc., 1969.

Bowman, William J. Graphic Communication. New York: John Wiley & Sons, Inc., 1968.

Chase's Calendar of Annual Events. Flint, Mich.: The Apple Tree Press, annual.

Coplan, Kate. Effective Library Exhibits. Dobbs Ferry, N.Y.: Oceana, 1974.

Dance, James C. "Public Relations for the Smaller Library," No. 4, Small Libraries Publications. Chicago: American Library Association, 1979.

Edsall, Marian S. "The Harried Librarian's Guide to Public Relations Resources." Madison, Wis.: The Coordinated Library Information Program, Inc., 1976.

Foster, Edith. "The Library in the Small Community," No. 14, Small Libraries Project LAD/ALA. Chicago: American Library Association, 1967.

Fruehling, Rosemary T. and Sharon Bouchard. The Art of Writing Effective Letters. New York: McGraw, 1972.

Glick, Nada Beth and Filomena Simora, ed. The Bowker Annual of Library & Book Trade Information. New York: R.R. Bowker Co., annual.

Harrison, K.C. Public Relations for Librarians. Grafton Basic Texts, Evelyn J.A. Evans, ed. London: André Deutsch Ltd., 1973.

Horn, George F. Visual Communication: Bulletin Boards, Exhibits, Visual Aids. Worcester, Mass.: Davis Publications, Inc., 1973.

Howard, Edward N. Local Power and the Community Library. No. 18, The Public Library Reporter. Chicago: American Library Association, 1978.

Illinois Library Association. "Funding of Public Libraries ... Some Dollar Stretching Techniques." Chicago: ILA, 1979.

Jacobs, Herbert. Practical Publicity: A Handbook for Public and Private Workers. New York: McGraw-Hill, 1964.

Krueger, Karen, ed. Illinois Libraries Vol. 60, No. 10. Springfield, Ill.: Illinois State Library, December 1978.

Mauger, Emily M. Modern Display Techniques. New York: Fairchild Publications, Inc., 1969.

Moore, H. Frazier and Bertand R. Canfield. Public Relations: Principles, Cases and Problems, 7th ed. Homewood, Ill.: Richard D. Irwin, Inc., 1977.

Moran, Irene, ed. The Library Public Relations Recipe Book. Chicago: American Library Association, 1978.

Rowe, Frank A. Display Fundamentals: A Basic Display Manual. Cincinnati, Ohio: The Display Publishing Co., 1965.

Rackow, Leo. Postercraft. New York: Sterling, 1971.

Sherman, Steve. ABC's of Library Promotion. Metuchen, N.J.: Scarecrow Press, 1980.

Siegel, Gonnie McClung. How to Advertise and Promote Your Small Business. New York: John Wiley & Sons, Inc., 1978.

Van Uchelen, Rod. Paste-Up: Production Techniques and New Applications. New York: Van Nostrand Reinhold Co., 1976.

Vereinigung Schweizerischer Bibliothekare. Bibliotheken in der Schweiz. Bern: 1976.

Walcott, Marian. "Telling the Library Story", No. 15, Small Libraries Project, LAD/ALA. Chicago: American Library Association, 1967.

Warncke, Ruth. Planning Library Workshops and Institutes, No. 17, Public Library Reporters. Chicago: American Library Association, 1976.

PERIODICALS

Library Journal. New York: R.R. Bowker Co., monthly.

Library PR News. Bloomfield, N.J.: Library Educational Institute, Inc., 6 issues per year.

School Library Journal. New York: R.R. Bowker Co., monthly.

Tips From Clip. Madison, Wis.: Coordinated Library Information Program, Inc., out-of-print.

Wilson Library Bulletin. New York: H.W. Wilson Co., monthly.

INDEX